# Surviving the Crisis of Motherhood

# Surviving the Crisis of Motherhood

Strategies for Caring for Your Child —
and Yourself
Paula Lubke Kollstedt

Cover and book design by Julie Lonneman
Photographs by L. Peter Edles

SBN 0-912228-91-1

# Contents

# A Word From the Author

This book is about being the mother of young children: what makes it good and what makes it bad, what makes it hurt and what makes it comfortable. But most of all, this book is about what makes it work—the mother herself.

My qualifications for writing this book are Kelly (12 years old), Lance (10), Stacey (six), and Jonathan (two).

My children are important to me for many reasons.

They are important here because they add reality to the research. For too long now we have had non-mother professionals giving mothers advice. And too often the result is a work of fiction.

This doesn't imply that biological birth bestows some magical parental wisdom. On the contrary, "motherhood as instinct" is one of the most frightening myths around. Such a theory says a mother doesn't have the right to be frustrated when awakened for the third time the same night by a screaming infant. At 4 a.m. she may not know what she thinks, but she does know what she feels—and it isn't motherly.

I didn't receive a B.A. in Mothering. There is no such thing, and if there were I'm sure I would never have chosen that career. After all, who would subject themselves to Diaper Changing 102, Rectal Thermometer Technique 205 and Oatmeal Preparation 409?

As a sophisticated college freshman, I thought a baby was something your mother had. Of course I might have one some day. (I might get appendicitis too!) I considered motherhood very little at all. A profession? Certainly not. Doctor, lawyer, indian chief—those were professions.

Upon graduation from college I thought I would go for my Ph.D., get a tan and save the Third World at the same time. Then I had a baby.

Then I also had buckets of soggy diapers, strained spinach on my white velvet blazer, not much of a tan—but lots of heat rash to contend with. At times I felt the Third World was much closer to being saved than my sanity.

I wondered if my career would suffer when I didn't go back to work; I wondered if my baby would suffer when I did. I thought of how I used to speak with confidence in a boardroom full of people, and how I now sometimes had difficulty speaking in complete sentences. I looked around the house and could see only mass confusion, and yet I knew I must have done something— I was so *tired*.

I had been told my life was my own, and yet I knew the look on my baby's face when I walked into a room. I missed having hours to spend reading, sleeping late on Saturday mornings, time to think without interruption and to share long philosophic conversations about the meaning of life after death. After three months of colic, four months of teething pain and one of the worst cases of chicken pox my pediatrician had ever seen, I began to question the meaning of life after birth—for the mother involved. Would I, could I survive the crisis of motherhood?

This book originated in life, my own, and the lives of mothers and fathers who have participated in my "Parenthood: Coping and Growing Workshops." An important amount of the material in this book comes from personal interviews with medical and management professionals.

Published sources are listed at the end of the first chapter to which they pertain. These references are by no means a complete or even representative survey of the thousands of books available on parenthood, human psychology and business management. For further information on source material listed, I refer readers to the bibliographies which many of the works referenced here include.

I welcome correspondence from any reader who would like to share ideas, criticisms, or experiences.

# Acknowledgments

It is difficult to appreciate the importance of acknowledgments until you write your own book.

Sincerest thanks to the mothers and fathers who have participated in "Parenthood: Coping and Growing Workshops." The insights of those parents continue to enrich my understanding and the understanding of others with whom they share experiences. Such sharing strengthens us because it makes us confident that there are as many ways to parent as there are parents.

Sincerest thanks to my friends and colleagues—all of them—but especially to Nina Thomas for her enthusiasm, diligent research and professional as well as personal support; to Jane and David Ruhmkorff, Dr. Virginia Quinn, Jim Thomas, Elsie Sprague, Peter Edles, Dave Smith and the staff of St. Anthony Messenger Press, especially to editors Karen Hurley and Carol Luebering for their expertise, encouragement and belief in an idea.

Sincerest thanks to my family—all of them—but especially to my parents, Mary and Elmer Lubke, and to my sister, Mary Ellen Barry, for *always* being there; to my husband, Steve Kollstedt, whose positive and energetic approach to living greatly influenced this project; and to my children, who helped me and hugged me. Without them this book would never have been written.

The very fact that our society does train initiates formally for most jobs...makes woman's role archaic and atypical in that women still learn by doing. They take on the vital, creative, important, central concern of their lives, which matters so much to everyone (they are assured), with very little advice or background. New mothers are expected to act by instinct; and this expectation in itself sets them apart from the rest of society, where people assume that they will be taught the basic rules of the jobs they have to do.

—Elizabeth Janeway
*Man's World, Woman's Place*

# Chapter 1
# Motherhood:
# The Social Complications

Motherhood in America today is confusing, if not devastating. We are faced with dozens of complicated issues: How do we feel good about doing a job for which we have never been trained? How do we deal with the loneliness and isolation of modern suburbia? Should we continue to work or stay home with the baby—and for how long? On whom do we call for help—and how do we admit that we need or deserve that help?

1

How do we handle the stresses of constant child care? Can we really fulfill our children's needs as well as our own? Why do we get so many headaches? And why are we feeling guilty, anxious and depressed? Will we ever be able to finish a conversation with our husband before 9 p.m.—and if we do, what will we say? What do we really want to do? And why are there never enough hours in the day to do it?

Sure we are mothers, but what does that really mean? And who ever said parenthood comes naturally anyway?

Certainly not mothers!

Mothers today live in the midst of radical social changes which affect the way we deal with our children and ourselves. The job of "mom" crashes in on most of us after we have had little more preparation for it than the first two chapters of Dr. Spock and our own experience of childhood—most of which we forgot long ago. Because of the small nuclear (two-generation) family, few young women serve an apprenticeship in caring for infants and children. So when the baby comes, we are scared.

Then, too, our understanding of what it means to be women is challenged. Americans have talked a lot about equality in marriage and more liberated roles for women, but research shows that couples become much more traditional with the birth of their first child. It is then that the husband becomes "breadwinner" and the wife becomes "mother."

In addition to confusions about women's roles, the family itself is in turmoil. The divorce rate has doubled in the last 10 years: Two of every five children born in the 80's will live in single-parent homes for at least part of their youth. The number of households headed by women increased more than one-third in the 70's, more than doubled in one generation. More than one-half of all mothers of school-age and preschool children work outside the home.

A mother's role is no longer defined. In the 50's we were told that total fulfillment is found as wife and mother. Today we are told total fulfillment is found only within ourselves, and that often means something more than mothering alone. Yet we must reconcile the new ethic which may include a paying job with the old ethic which says mothering is a full-time job.

No matter what a woman decides, when she has a baby there are always new concerns. Women often have difficulty coping with the added responsibility of this new life, the loss of togetherness as a couple, the increased housekeeping tasks, the sheer physical exhaustion.

Motherhood has had some bad press. Medea and the Oedipus complex we can handle. What is tough is being mentioned in the same breath with apple pie and the American flag. The job of mother is complicated by all the mythology. There is the Serene Madonna, the Jewish mother, the Italian mother, mother-love, Mother Goose, the mother on *The Brady Bunch*. All are storybook stereotypes; all avoid reality like a mother protecting her young.

And yet as a profession, mothering is a non-job with little status in today's society. The U.S. Labor Department's *Dictionary of Occupational Titles* defines some 22,000 occupations on a scale which ranks "skill" from a high of one to a low of 887. Homemakers, foster mothers, child-care attendants and nursery school teachers rank 878th.

Obviously that rating didn't consider a recent study by the American Council of Life Insurance which said it is a good thing women at home caring for children don't charge directly for their services. If they did, according to this research, an average paycheck would come to $17,351.88 a year, conservatively speaking.

These figures were based on the wage scale of a large East Coast city and on the assumption that a mother at home performs her tasks about 100 hours a week, seven days a week. (The unions would be screaming.)

Weekly breakdown is as follows:

| | | |
|---|---|---|
| nursemaid | 45.1 hours @ $2.70: | $121.77 |
| dietician | 1.2 hours @ $4.00: | $4.80 |
| food buyer | 3.3 hours @ $2.70: | $8.91 |
| cook | 13.1 hours @ $3.50: | $45.85 |
| dishwasher | 6.2 hours @ $2.80: | $17.36 |
| housekeeper | 17.5 hours @ $4.50: | $78.75 |
| laundress | 5.9 hours @ $3.00: | $17.70 |
| seamstress | 1.3 hours @ $3.50: | $4.55 |
| maintenance person | 1.7 hours @ $3.50: | $5.95 |
| gardener | 2.3 hours @ $3.50: | $8.05 |
| chauffeur | 2.0 hours @ 10.00: | $20.00 |

Grand total $333.69

Overall, our 99.6-hour work week is worth $333.69, and that does not consider double-digit inflation. Add the fact that women at home contribute never less than one sixth, often at least one quarter of the gross national product, and we might well drop the "only" when we say a woman is a homemaker.

Money talks. But the wages just discussed are theoretical. Husbands do not really pay their wives $333.69 every week for services rendered, and so mothers and their contributions are disavowed by a dollar-oriented society.

## Lack of Training

One important institution which has chalked off family life with a felt eraser is the school, which prepares people for every career except parenthood. Idealistic educators go around with their heads in the clouds while mothers go around with their feet in the cereal.

High schools and colleges as a general rule consider family life and the role of mother little more than a natural instinct for nesting. They forget that the survival of humanity rests with families, and families must be maintained carefully through art and science—art and science which few of us have the opportunity to develop as children in the family unit.

So mothers are abandoned by the teachers they emulate. Suddenly Mom is her own boss even though she has never studied the business. She is on her own without so much as a Friday morning board meeting of her contemporaries with whom to check reality. Mothers suffer, children suffer, society suffers.

It is claimed that women are notorious talkers ("If you want to spread the word, tell it to a woman"). And yet motherhood is one of the best kept secrets of womankind. Probably because of the low esteem in which society holds motherhood, few women document what they have learned. How did other women deal with an infant who wouldn't sleep? A toddler who wouldn't take "no" for an answer? A hyperactive four-year-old?

Most importantly, women don't share how to take care of *themselves* once they become mothers. Writer Geneva Hickman explains the difficulties:

> Mothers of young children should not neglect themselves.... Proper diet is important and can be arranged if you plan ahead. Arise and have breakfast before the baby's 6 a.m. feeding. Lunch

5

will have to be a sandwich that you can eat while you fold the laundry. Dinner should be a hot meal you prepare for your husband and yourself. Eat it leisurely and have a pleasant conversation. At first you may find it difficult to enjoy your frozen TV dinners with all that screaming from the nursery....

When you go out with the girls in the evening (at least once a week), pay attention to your appearance. No matter how frantic your exit may be, before you leave you must ask yourself three questions: (1) Is all the oatmeal brushed from my hair? (2) Did I put on my dress? (3) Do I remember where I'm going?

But often it's not a laughing matter. Experienced mothers are disregarded as resources. No one is working on mothers' problems and no one can actually solve the problems except mothers themselves. Unfortunately, women don't often share these vital issues.

## Isolation

One young mother tells the story of having attended an all-female high school and college where she was accustomed to an intellectual, problem-solving exchange among women. She expected it. But when she got into the real world, it wasn't that way.

At a gathering of neighbors she would say, "The baby's not sleeping through the night."

And they would say, "Don't worry, that's just the way it is."

She would say, "But he doesn't even sleep well during the day. He takes 10-minute naps every two hours."

And they would say, "Oh, he does? Mine never did that." Or, "Gee, I've never heard of one doing that."

She felt isolated. She felt lonely. And for the first

time she felt alienated from the very group she had trusted for so long.

Are all these "Serene Madonnas" in conspiracy? Probably not. But as children grow older, a marvelous kind of amnesia sets in so that experienced mothers remember only the good things. No one bothers to recall and document a non-job, let alone try to teach other, newer mothers what, after all, comes naturally. The result may be a delightful memory bank for the individual, but such forgetfulness is certainly no help to society.

Writer Jamie Coy Wallace describes it this way:

> Ha! After two weeks of pacing the bedroom with a colicky baby, with hardly time to wash my hair, much less do decoupage, I knew I'd been gulled, grossly underestimating the responsibilities of mothering. How, I wondered, could I have ever believed the soothing fictions fed mothers-to-be? Why didn't anyone tell me how bereft I'd feel without the stimulation of office work and colleagues? Even my own mother neglected to mention how trying it is to have to be *everything* to one tiny human being....
>
> The truth—which I had to find out by *myself*— is that a mother, without benefit of nurse or nanny, can *never* cease to care about (and worry about) her child; and, for the first few years, she must be physically *with* him practically all the time. You are an infant's whole world, and this terrifying responsibility can't be suspended, even if you *do* have flu, cramps and a hangover.

Sociologists say many women are rebelling at the way society today institutionalizes motherhood. Women love their children but they hate motherhood. In sociologist Jessie Bernard's words, "They object to the isolation in which they must perform the role of mother, cut off from help, from one another, from the outside world. For the first time they are protesting the false aura of romanticism with which motherhood is endowed...."

Dr. Bernard calls depression "the characteristic illness of married women today." This depression can be so bad as to lead to suicide. According to the Reverend Kenneth B. Murphy of Rescue, Inc., a non-profit, nonsectarian organization affiliated with Harvard University, Massachusetts General Hospital and the Boston City Hospitals, more suicide attempts will be made in a given year by housewives who stay home to care for their children than any other occupational group in the United States.

Researchers say we mothers are in crisis because we were part of a generation of little girls socialized to believe they would love motherhood but who, indeed, had no idea what motherhood was all about.

## Myths of Motherhood

Our society heaps on the propaganda, and that includes many myths beginning with the old stand-by, "Motherhood is the most natural thing in the world." Some others include:

1) *A mother must be able to fulfill all of her child's needs.* If this were true, every mother would be a dismal failure at some point in her career. Different mothering skills are needed at different stages of a child's growth— and for different children. The total provider who is an excellent mother for the helpless infant may be limiting to the exploring toddler, damaging to the teen struggling for independence, and a comfort to the sick child of any age.

As one mother said, "Every time you master the game, the rules change." Mothering comes naturally at one point and is a lot of hard work at another. Different people would define the good and bad times differently, but no single woman is going to be a perfect mother for a given child at every stage of life. And that is O.K.—that is human.

2) *Motherhood bestows its own infinite supply of patience.* What else could have made the madonnas so serene? Surely it wasn't the 2 a.m. feedings, the milk allergy, or the baby's 103° fever just before Mom is scheduled to serve Thanksgiving dinner to 25 guests.

The fact is that patience, like parenthood, takes time and experience. Indeed, patience may even be more difficult for mothers to achieve than for other professionals because of the frustration we feel performing a job for which we have never been trained.

Our society, which would never dream of sending a bus driver to work without his driver's license or a surgeon to the operating room without special training—many years of it—every day allows mothers to give birth without the slightest idea of the skills involved in nurturing a child. Somehow we are supposed to acquire this knowledge by some magical maternal osmosis. Unfortunately, the only miracle which occurs at birth is that of life itself.

3) *Having a baby will help your marriage.* If you buy this you obviously have not as yet given birth to your first child. A baby is doubtless one of the niftiest creations God and the two of you will ever come up with, but care and maintenance of that creation takes its toll in time, energy and emotion. Things will change. That is both a threat and a promise, but the happiest parents are those who learn to change with the territory instead of longing for what used to be.

4) *I won't be a good mother because I'm not good with other people's children.* There are no children like

yours. Every mother knows that, and every mother knows how much understanding of childhood her own children help her develop.

Some of us, however, absolutely are not and never will be wonderful with kids. But that is not bad, because we are wonderful at other things and our children will benefit.

5) *Mothers aren't sexy.* Want to bet? Sure there are new concerns, new responsibilities, but new maturity can happen as well (more about that in Chapter 2). Childbirth and breastfeeding can make a woman more aware of her body, and so make her more sexually responsive.

In the book *Our Bodies, Ourselves*, a new mother commented, "Having my first child was the first experience in my life in which I felt my physical being was as important as my mind. I related to my total body. I became very unselfconscious. I felt my body as a fantastic machine."

6) *Motherhood is a woman's total fulfillment; women were born to be mothers.* And if we were meant to fly we would have been born with wings! So much for that logic.

People were born to be human beings. From that point on fulfillment in life is a matter of choice, prayer, talent, guts and hard work. Life is what we make it. The secret to success is knowing what we want so that we can turn dreams into reality.

It also means understanding that nobody is a perfectly fulfilled *anything*. Excellence in mothering is not a matter of chemical bonding. It is a matter of learning the skills which contribute to a child's total growth— those skills which are needed to nurture a loving, confident, independent person.

7) *Motherhood is the hardest job in the world; it*

*requires total selflessness.* Hey, nothing is *that* bad. Motherhood is filled with moments of great joy. There are first smiles, first steps, first hugs. Remember, though, hugs at just the right moment cannot always be counted on, and that can be a disappointment.

Motherhood can give an inner direction, a sense of purpose, a link to the Source of all life. Non-stop anything, however, is a drudge, and it is important to remember that in order to love our children we must first love ourselves. An all-give relationship can only end in heartache for someone, perhaps everyone.

8) *Motherhood is an intellectual wasteland; mothers are boring.* Society may dictate the myths, but women do not have to make them come true. A braggart is always a bore whether she is talking about her two-year-old or her brilliant summation to the jury.

When mothers do talk about their young children, it is probably a fair guess that little honest communication actually occurs. That, after all, is an outgrowth of our original myth, "Being a mother is the most natural thing in the world." The truth is that mothers do not often tell what it is like to live with preschoolers.

## The Women's Movement and Mothering

Mothers can ignore society's attempts at brainwashing, but it is hard to ignore society itself. Society is our environment; it has shaped us into the persons that we are. Certainly we cannot discuss society's influence on motherhood without mentioning the women's movement, very much a fact of life in contemporary American society. Most women are neither Gloria Steinem nor Phyllis Schlafly. But we are human beings with important considerations about the issues of the day. And motherhood is one issue we know intimately.

What impact has the philosophy of the women's movement had on motherhood? Plenty.

The negative impact gets lots of coverage. Militant feminist thought has been blamed by some for everything from juvenile delinquency to the demise of the family. But the women's movement has also had a much less-examined positive force on motherhood.

Feminists have added to the status of mothers by offering women options. These options, like a paying job, are not necessarily better than working full-time at home raising children, especially in the preschool years. But in turning down other alternatives in favor of full-time motherhood, a woman gives new worth to that role. We are not raising our young children because we *have* to, we are raising them because we *want* to.

Another aspect of the women's movement is sisterhood: camaraderie among women. Man have had it for years—on the football field, at the office, in the bar. Men were expected to get along. Women, on the other hand, were expected to be jealous and vindictive. "Lord help the sister, who comes between me and my man," they sang.

Today women have a new rhetoric, a new sense of sharing. One proof of it is the book you are reading right now. In the 50's no one would ever have suggested that mothers might look at their own sense of identity; back then it was assumed that marriage and motherhood were all the identity any of us needed.

Libbers have forced society to redefine true femininity. Dr. Niles Newton says, "The woman who is adequate in her female role must be active, productive, capable of concerted effort." This view of femininity is quite the opposite of that submissive flower dressed in petticoats many of us faced in the mirror during grade school.

Margaret Mead wrote, "The natural rhythms of the female in our society are primarily considered a nuisance and a handicap, to be muted, transcended or ignored. In other societies pregnancy is not disguised; breastfeeding is an open and casual act."

Even today men are primarily the obstetricians and pediatricians who guide us through childbirth and childrearing. Of course the answer is not a population of "female only" OB's and children's doctors, but rather a professional population which is sensitive to the insights mothers have to offer. Candor undoubtedly leads to fewer incidences of terrifying childbirth and traumatic child care. Such communication will give women the confidence to mother *their* way, and feel good about it.

As women grow in self-esteem, they can take another look at men. By shattering the myths about what is feminine, we shatter myths about masculinity as well. Women may want to experience the workplace more fully; men may want to experience the children more fully. Creative living alternatives allow both sexes to be more fully human.

But whether we choose some new style or remain more traditional, the choice can be our own. Women have finally come of age—chronologically, psychologically, spiritually. Such adulthood challenges each individual to find out what makes her most free, most fulfilled, most herself.

Such re-creation is not a selfish goal: It can be a lonely and painful journey on the way to self-possession. But in the end it will benefit us and everyone whose life we touch.

As Judith Viorst said some time ago, "Without this interior journey, I fear, we will merely be trading old myths for new. Without this lonely battle no husband, no child, no job in all the world can give us ourselves."

Mothers are in process in today's society. We challenge what has been; we look forward to what will be. In the meantime we are beginning to take one of the most important steps on the road to change. We are beginning to take control of our own lives. And that, in itself, makes mothering a lot less complicated.

## For Discussion and Awareness

1) In what ways do you find your role as mother confusing? What conflicts do you personally face as a mother?

2) Did you receive any training for your job as mother? How do you feel about that?

3) How do you answer when someone asks, "What do you do?" Are you comfortable with that answer?

4) When do you find motherhood isolating? How do you cope with that isolation?

5) Before you had children, what were your own personal myths about motherhood? What kind of mother did you imagine you would be? What myths of motherhood are you still holding onto?

6) How has the women's movement affected your life? In your view, what effect has feminism had on the modern American family?

## Idea for Action

Keep a journal of your experiences as a mother and how you solved problems at various stages of your child's development. You can refer to the journal if you have other children, use it when consulting with other mothers, and save it for your children to use as a reference when they get older.

## Bibliography

Bernard, Jessie. *The Future of Motherhood.* New York: Dial, 1974.
  *The Future of Marriage.* New York: Bantam Books, 1973.
Boston Women's Health Book Collective. *Our Bodies, Ourselves.* New York: Simon and Schuster, 1971.
Chess, Stella, M.D., *et al. Your Child Is a Person.* New York: Penguin Books, 1977.
Dodson, Fitzhugh, M.D. *How to Parent.* New York: Signet, 1971.
Hickman, Geneva. "Advice to New Mothers From a Used One." *Redbook* (December, 1968), pp. 56-57.
Janeway, Elizabeth. *Man's World, Woman's Place.* New York: William Morrow and Co., 1971.
Newton, Niles, Ph.D. *Maternal Emotions.* New York: Paul B. Hoeber, Inc., Harper and Brothers, 1977.
Nordheimer, Jon. "The Family in Transition: A Challenge From Within." *The New York Times* (November 27, 1977), p. 1.
Viorst, Judith. "What Worries Me Most About Women's Lib." *Redbook* (May, 1974), pp. 51-52.
Wallace, Jamie Coy. "Let's Demystify Motherhood." *Cosmopolitan* (May, 1975), p. 24.

A sophisticated view of human reality takes account of the possibility that where there is love, there is also some hate; where there is admiration, there is also some envy; where there is devotion, there is also some hostility; where there is success, there is also apprehension. It takes great wisdom to realize that all feelings are legitimate: the positive, the negative, and the ambivalent.

—Haim Ginott
*Between Parent and Child*

# Chapter 2
# Motherhood and Feelings

Motherhood is easy—if you don't have children.

Once you have them, whining, interruptions, confusion and dirty diapers *ad infinitum* are only the beginning of countless frustrations. "Motherhood is a mixed bag," as psychiatric nurse Angela Barron McBride says. It's an ambivalent role, and our feelings fluctuate accordingly. We yell, we scream, we stomp—and within minutes we are swept away by feelings of love.

Quite simply, motherhood is a crisis.

No matter what we have to do, no matter how badly we have to do it, the baby will not take care of herself. Even if we find competent day care for our children and become something besides a mother some of the time, that concern remains—usually with a runny nose and mud on her shoes.

Motherhood means crisis because motherhood means change. It is a high-risk career that is exhausting and continuous, sometimes boring, often fascinating and, on occasion, terrifying. It is a job that promises nothing and demands everything.

"I'm a mother," one woman said recently at a job interview. "I can handle anything: stress, responsibility, rigorous management problems, long hours on an assembly line. And," she added, "I'm not bad at riot control either."

## Surviving the Crisis

Parenthood, according to psychologists, can be the greatest crisis to befall a marriage. But, they add quickly, while a personal crisis may disrupt your life it can also be the best thing that ever happened to you.

Anthropologists Nena and George O'Neill explain that, in crisis, *change* is the survival word. Unless we learn to move through crisis without delay, there could be trouble.

The O'Neills suggest the following steps to help mothers—or anyone—move quickly but deliberately through crisis.

1) *Remember, it is not the nature of a crisis that determines its impact but, rather, our attitude toward it.*

Did you ever wonder how some people can manage to survive the impact of a trauma like the loss of a child or spouse while others fall apart over a run in their stocking? The key lies in attitude.

If before we had a child (or three or four of them), we thought we were in a "safe" place, we could be in for problems. If, on the other hand, we realized even before the children came that there is no such thing as a safe place, that life continually makes unexpected demands, the impact of a new family member will not be so great.

2) *Try not to panic.*

In the early months and years of a child's life, mothers feel many strains—fatigue, physical and psychological disequilibrium, low energy levels. Yet in spite of our own needs, we must deal with the intense demands of the young child as well as increased household responsibilities and continuing relationships with our husband, other children, relatives and friends.

Panic, the O'Neills warn, is a common reaction at this stage. Mothers both long for things as they used to be and agonize over what might have been—the "I-used-to-be-so-happy" syndrome.

The worst strategy is avoidance, denying problems exist. Mothers must, therefore, be willing to accept their negative feelings rather than suppress them so that change can begin.

One young mother had wanted a baby for as long as she could remember. When she married her high school sweetheart, they planned to begin a family right away, but it was nine years and many visits to specialists later that their first child was born.

"I hoped and prayed for this baby so long that my frustrations as a new mother took me completely by surprise," this mother confesses. "I love my baby, but in the early months there were times when he cried constantly—no matter what I did. I had little time for even my simplest personal needs.

"My husband travels in his job and I began to resent

the time he was gone," she continues. "Sometimes I even resented my baby for his unceasing demands. And yet I couldn't, or perhaps wouldn't, admit that resentment even to myself. I believed those feelings made me a bad mother."

That unwillingness to admit her negative feelings locked her even deeper into emotional crisis. It is easy to understand how, in the midst of such stresses, a mother may forget about herself, become run-down physically and susceptible to many illnesses she could easily fight off under other circumstances.

Thus the panic stage can be both physically and emotionally debilitating. But the sooner we recognize and accept what is happening, the more quickly we will pass through this phase.

3) *Remobilize resources with positive action toward solution.*

This is the period where we begin to shift gears and say yes to the reality of motherhood. As we become more comfortable with ourselves, we can begin to resolve the crisis and achieve growth.

We do not have to fear crisis. That is the crucial insight allowing growth under stress. "Go into a crisis, experiencing it fully," the O'Neills advise, "not avoiding it, not trying to diffuse it.... We may experience considerable discomfort at first, but those who come through crisis with real change and growth are often those who seem to take the crisis the hardest."

The O'Neills suggest a life *strategy*, not a life *plan*. Plans are static and predictable—but unfortunately not dependable. A contemporary blessedness is attached to anything planned. Parents announce with pride, "This is Michelle. She was a planned child." And everyone smiles. It is as if the plan itself will make them all live happily ever after.

A life strategy, on the other hand, has a built-in safety feature: Plan B. Strategies allow for alternatives—in case Plan A turns out differently than we thought it would. Such an open approach allows for the inevitable surprises in every life.

So it seems that even a crisis can have the positive side effect of growth for the individual. But there is one catch: Growth is never easy. Growth means change, and change can be difficult, even painful; but we do it nonetheless. We do it because change is exciting. It is a challenge. It adds meaning to our existence. To be alive at all involves some risk.

## Postpartem Depression

One typical risk of motherhood is postpartem depression. How the Serene Madonna managed to avoid it is still a mystery. One young mother tells how it hit her at the grocery store. She was standing at the meat counter when she suddenly burst into tears.

"Why," she asked, "should the sight of a pot roast cause me to break down and cry?" It was only later that she decided she had nothing personal against pot roasts, only against having to select one.

"After the fantastic miracle of birth I had been a part of only days before, the supermarket was such a comedown. I thought, 'What's a remarkable girl like you doing in a place like this?' I wanted the music to play on forever."

But it doesn't. Research indicates postpartem blues can occur and reoccur anytime within a year after delivery, and even later. The first stage, according to researchers, comes just after the baby's birth as we move from the incredible high of the birth to the incredible low of burning stitches, constipation, sore breasts and general weariness.

The second stage of depression may last from one to three months. It is triggered by the actual coping with a newborn at home. While Dad goes back to work and the world goes on turning, Mom is left to deal with colic, night feedings, indescribable fatigue and explaining to our toddler how nice it is to have a new sister.

The third stage involves long-term adjustments to new motherhood and can last up to a year or more. "Often we remain upset months after the baby's birth," explains the book *Our Bodies, Ourselves*, "because we expected at some point to get our lives and feelings back to 'normal.' It is important to understand that once we become mothers we will never again lead altogether the same lives."

Feelings are tricky. They are much more a matter of circumstance than will. So if you are grabbed by a feeling you don't like, try to minimize—not deny—it. That feeling is not your fault. Your responsibility lies in what you *do* with the feeling.

"One day the baby cried for what seemed like hours," said Carol, the mother of a five-month-old. "He cried and cried until I couldn't stand it anymore. I screamed at him, 'Shut up! What more can I do for you? What more do you want from me?'"

Carol's outburst to her baby was not just the result of one torturous afternoon of crying. It was also a result of the five months this new mother had cared for and worried about her child. It was the result of several nights of broken sleep because Carol had a bad cold and could hardly breathe. It was the result of a meeting earlier in the day with an old friend who had asked, "What have you been doing with your life?"

We can learn a great deal about ourselves from our feelings. Teacher and priest John Powell says, "The important thing is the realization that every emotional reaction is telling us something about ourselves.... When I do react emotionally, I know that not everyone would react as I have. Everyone does not have the same stored-up emotions which I have.... If I want to know something about myself, my needs, my self-image, my sensitivity, my psychological programming and my values, then I must listen very sensitively to my own emotions."

We need not apologize for our feelings. We need only deal with them positively. Perhaps we could use some time alone, some time away from our child to appreciate her specialness. We may need sleep and good food to get over a cold or to keep ourselves from getting one. Our feelings themselves may be intense, but we can ride them out, learn from them—and realize that somehow, someday, they will leave as quickly as they came.

## Basic Needs

In *The Family Book of Child Care*, Niles Newton describes emotions as drives, powers that make us move toward fulfillment of basic needs. She divides these needs into the following categories:

| | |
|---|---|
| breathing | avoiding pain |
| drinking | resting |
| eating | exercising |
| eliminating waste | sensory stimulation |
| avoiding irritating | sexual activity |
|    substances and poison | expelling a baby |
| loving and touching | expelling milk |

According to Dr. Newton, any person's happiness and security is dependent on the fulfillment of these needs. She cautions us never to approach a drowning man without a life preserver: He will pull you under with him. Well, according to my calculations, many a mother with an infant and/or preschoolers is "drowning" when it comes to fulfillment of her own basic needs.

Mothers usually have no problem breathing (since we can do that *plus* just about anything, and we always have to do at least two things at the same time). Avoiding irritating substances and poison is not much of a problem either, especially since we are very much involved with keeping our toddler from doing the same. When it comes to expelling a baby, we manage to take time for that, too, no matter what the rest of the world needs.

Almost all the remaining needs described as vital for well-being can, however, be difficult for the mother of young children to satisfy personally. Water, food, exercise and sleep for the mother all become secondary to meeting those needs in the helpless child. Happily, the baby himself assists the mother in fulfilling two of the drives: touching with love and expelling milk. (The La Leche League can help here too, by providing vital supporting assistance to the nursing mother.) But any mother knows that personal time for something as basic as expelling waste is absolute luxury. And when a person considers going to the bathroom a luxury, you can imagine how far down the list sensory stimulation and sexual activity can get.

### Stress

In short, a mother's life is filled with stress. Ogden Tanner, researcher for Time-Life Books says, "To a scientist, stress is any action or situation that places special physical or psychological demands upon a person—anything that can unbalance his individual equilibrium."

Stress is everywhere, and it can come in the form of

good or bad news. Getting fired causes stress, but so does getting a promotion. Getting a divorce is stressful, but so is getting married.

Psychiatrists Thomas H. Holmes and Richard Rahe of the University of Washington School of Medicine researched stress for 20 years and compiled the following social readjustment scale, which has proven useful in predicting illness which may result from stress.

To figure your score, think of your life for the past 12 months and give yourself the point value for any event which has occurred within that time.

### Predicting Stress-Related Illness

| Event | Value of Impact |
|---|---|
| Death of spouse | 100 |
| Divorce | 73 |
| Marital separation | 65 |
| Jail term | 63 |
| Death of a close family member | 63 |
| Personal injury or illness | 53 |
| Marriage | 50 |
| Being fired from a job | 47 |
| Marital reconciliation | 45 |
| Retirement | 45 |
| Change in health of a family member | 44 |
| Pregnancy | 40 |
| Sex difficulties | 39 |
| Gain of a new family member | 39 |
| Business readjustment | 39 |
| Change in financial state | 38 |
| Death of close friend | 37 |
| Change to different line of work | 36 |
| Change in number of arguments with spouse | 35 |
| Mortgage or loan over $10,000 | 31 |

Foreclosure of mortgage or loan ............ 30
Change in responsibilities at work .......... 29
Son or daughter leaving home .............. 29
Trouble with in-laws ...................... 29
Outstanding personal achievement .......... 28
Wife begins or stops work ................. 26
Begin or end school ...................... 26
Change in living conditions ................. 25
Revision of personal habits ................. 24
Trouble with boss ......................... 23
Change in hours or conditions ............. 20
Change in residence ...................... 20
Change in schools ........................ 20
Change in recreation ...................... 19
Change in church activities ................ 19
Change in social activities ................. 18
Mortgage or loan less than $10,000 ......... 17
Change in sleeping habits ................. 16
Change in number of family get-togethers .... 15
Change in eating habits ................... 15
Vacation ................................. 13
Christmas ............................... 12
Minor violations of the law ................ 11

If your total for the year is under 150, you probably won't have any adverse reaction. A score of 150-199 indicates a mild problem, with a 34 percent chance you will feel the impact of stress with physical symptoms. From 200 to 299, you qualify as having a moderate problem, with a 51 percent chance of experiencing a change in your health. A score of over 300 could lead to a serious change in your health.

Consider the fact that in a single year a woman might marry (50), move into a new house (20), become pregnant (40), gain a new family member (39), change to a different line of work (36), stop work (26—they mean, of course, stop work *outside* the home; as usual, motherhood itself is not categorized as work), revise personal habits (24), change sleeping habits (16), change recreational habits (19), and change social activities (18). Add Christmas (12) and you have a grand total of 300 points!

And they scoffed when Helen Reddy sang, "I am strong, I am invincible, I am woman."

Yet, a word of hope: Most recent studies show that people who live in the "rat race" often live longer than those who exist in a reasonably placid, if boring, world. A vital pace keeps your system going. The person living in so-called peace gets no practice at handling stress. The first stressful situation may greatly harm her.

Some stress is vital to well-being. The secret is in knowing how much stress is right for you—and how to handle it.

What is your unique reaction to stress, and is it appropriate? The following is a self-test, devised to predict the kinds of problems excessive stress can cause, according to personality type.

### Testing Personal Stress Reactions

Your two older children have just arrived home from school and both start talking at the same time. The paperman rings the doorbell and asks to be paid. The baby starts crying as your three-year-old drops a jar of orange juice which breaks all over the kitchen floor. The dog runs away when you open the door to pay the paper bill. Then the phone rings. The call is from your son's teacher who says she needs to talk with you "immediately" about your son's misbehavior in school. What do you do? Think about it for a minute.

- If you just look at the children and say, "This place is like Grand Central Station today!," then begin to handle one thing at a time, you are one of the *placid* types who will probably live to a ripe old age.
- If your reaction is: "I'd walk out, slam the door, and chuck it all for a one-way ticket to Tahiti," you are an *excessive reactor* who, researchers say, is prone to coronaries, degenerative arthritis and ulcers.
- If you would do nothing, simply suppressing your feelings, perhaps not even aware that you are under stress, you are a *deficient reactor* who tends toward skin outbreaks, rheumatoid arthritis and colitis.
- If, though aware of your feelings, you would say nothing, you are a *restrained reactor*, and you are most likely to get diabetes, hyperthyroidism, hypertension, asthma and migraine.

Now the purpose of this exercise is not to bring on a tension headache. It is simply an attempt to raise our awareness of the family situations in which stress, improperly handled, can do damage to our bodies as well as our minds.

If we are restrained reactors who rarely admit or act on our own valid feelings, are we destined to stay that way? If we react excessively to the stresses of parenthood, must we face ulcers and coronaries? Of course not. We can learn creative coping.

### Guerrilla Tactics for Mothers

Although we may not have control over the stresses we must face, we do have control over our own reactions to stress. Certain behaviors can go a long way to change our attitudes and relieve stress at the same time. These tips on creative coping might be called "guerrilla tactics for mothers":

1) *Keep in the best possible physical shape.* Try to avoid nicotine, excessive caffeine and carbohydrates. One mother we know was having trouble sleeping at night. It never occurred to her that the eight cups of coffee she drinks every day might have something to do with it.

Remember that exercise is good for your mind as well as your body. According to cardiovascular specialists, vigorous walking is one of the best exercises there is. And that is something we can do with the baby in the stroller, no uniform required.

2) *Keep in the best possible spiritual shape.* Make a space for prayer and reflection, then use it regularly. Some mothers join a prayer group or read the Gospels (Luke is a good place to start); others learn to meditate, do yoga, or seek out a spiritual advisor they can really talk to.

But whatever you do, remember that Mary was a mother too, and she showed us how our whole life can be a prayer. Soothing the baby at midnight, watching the children play in the yard, handling our feelings well—these are all prayers. Life is filled with opportunities to become more loving, to answer God's call to be all that we are meant to be. Or, as one mother put it, "to love unconditionally in these messy concrete circumstances."

3) *Keep cool.* Think, "In a hundred years what difference will it make?"

4) *Have a good friend with whom you can talk honestly on a regular basis.* This means a friend *besides* your husband and preferably another mother. This person should be someone who loves you as you are, but who encourages you to grow.

5) *Simplify your life.* Stop doing three things at one time. Get out of the house (if only for a walk) at least twice a day.

6) *Seek information from others.* Take a class. Always be ready for a new idea. Even the young mother sitting next to you on the park bench may be as eager to talk to you as you are to her.

7) *Take some time just for yourself*—at least one hour a day. Schedule that time just as surely as you schedule dinner and the baby's nap. Then make it happen. This is *your* time to refresh and renew, which is something that everybody (even Supermom) needs.

8) *Go to bed*—if it is late. Things always look bleakest at midnight. Convince yourself you will worry about it in the morning. (I promise you will forget.)

9) *Get up and get with it*—if it is not late. Sometimes the idea of a task is much worse than the task itself. If it is important to you, you will feel better when you have done it. If it is not important, forget about it and do something that is.

10) *Meet your husband for lunch.* Talking with him in the middle of the day when you are both optimistic and on top of things is marvelous.

11) *Have a good cry.* Remember football player Rosey Grier singing Carol Hall's song on the television special *Free to Be You and Me:*

> It's all right to cry.
> Crying gets the sad out of you.
> It's all right to cry.
> It might make you feel better.

12) *Set priorities.* Procrastinate only when it is a deliberate decision.

13) *Take a hot bath.* Ahh....

14) *Don't feel bad about saying no.* Parents are stewards of God's favorite growing things—children—but not without strings attached. Stewardship demands responsibility. For parents that means managing our

children's behavior. Consistent, loving discipline includes both the words *yes* and *no*.

15) *Like yourself.* Then the above list will make a lot of sense.

An important part of surviving the crisis of motherhood and coping with stress lies in understanding ourselves and what is happening to us while our children are young. It is easy to see the changes taking place in children as they develop. The changes unfolding in mothers are less visible, but no less dramatic. We are maturing, growing in ways we never dreamed existed. It is simply a matter of accepting our children as an inevitable, irreplaceable part of our growth.

## For Discussion and Awareness

1) Was the crisis of motherhood a shock to you? How could you have been better prepared for motherhood?

2) Did you experience postpartem depression? What do you remember about it?

3) Are you good at handling your feelings? Explain.

4) Which of the basic needs listed in this chapter do you have difficulty meeting? Why?

5) What are the most stressful aspects of motherhood for you personally? Name a stress that you handle well. Name a stress that you have trouble handling.

6) Which of the "guerrilla tactics" for mothers could most benefit you in learning to cope creatively?

## Idea for Action

Gather a group of parents together regularly for an "executive board meeting" to find solutions to problems, discuss goals and examine priorities. Begin your meetings with each person in the group telling their "good news" and "bad news" since the last meeting. Such sharing will identify areas of growth as well as problems which other parents in the group may be able to help solve.

## Bibliography

Ginott, Haim G. *Between Parent and Child*. New York: Avon Books, 1969.

McBride, Angela Barron. *The Growth and Development of Mothers*. New York: Harper and Row, 1974.

Newton, Niles. *The Family Book of Child Care*. New York: Harper and Row, 1957.

O'Neill, Nena and George. *Shifting Gears*. New York: Avon Books, 1975.

Powell, John. *The Secret of Staying in Love*. Niles, Illinois: Argus Communications, 1974.

Tanner, Ogden, *et. al. Stress*. New York: Time-Life Books, 1976.

Thomas, Marlo. *Free to Be You and Me*. New York: McGraw Hill, 1974.

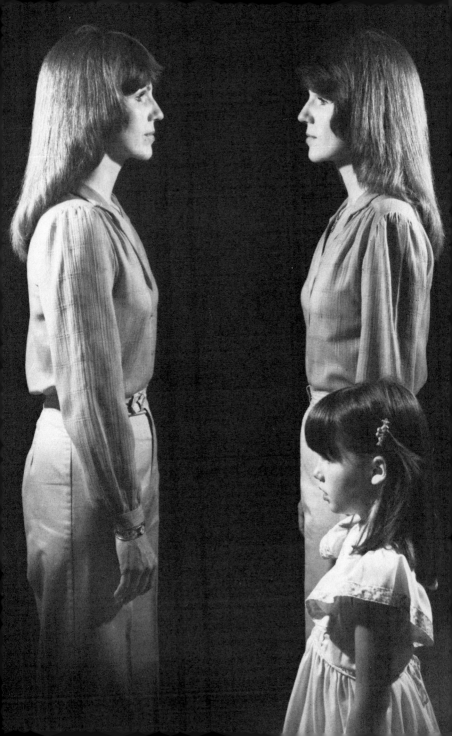

Last year I had a shampoo and set every
   week and
Slept an unbroken sleep beneath the
   Venetian chandelier of our discerningly
   eclectic bedroom, but
This year we have a nice baby,
And Gerber's strained bananas in my hair,
And gleaming beneath the Venetian
   chandelier,
A diaper pail, a portacrib, and him,
A nice baby, drooling on our antique
   satin spread
While I smile and say how nice. It is often
   said
That motherhood is very maturing.

   —Judith Viorst
      *It's Hard to Be Hip Over Thirty and
      Other Tragedies of Married Life*


# Chapter 3
# Mother: Parent vs. Person

Motherhood is no ego trip.

After we have dedicated months—even years—of
our fullest concentration to parenthood, the product of
that dedication still throws temper tantrums regularly in
church and screams for candy in the supermarket
check-out line. At which point we are confronted by the
cold stares of a hostile group of fellow human beings
who have apparently forgotten that their children (or

35

they themselves) ever acted that way.

How confident are you in the face of such adversity? The following questionnaire can give some indication. Check the block which most appropriately explains your feelings about the statement.

## Mother's Attitude Inventory

|  | Agree | Undecided | Disagree |
|---|---|---|---|
| 1) When I do something just for me, I feel selfish. | | | |
| 2) It is normal for mothers to have both positive and negative feelings toward their children. | | | |
| 3) Right now life presents me with many options and alternatives. | | | |
| 4) I believe I have more trouble coping than most mothers. | | | |
| 5) There is no one "right way" to mother. | | | |
| 6) I should give some thought to what I want to be doing five years from now. | | | |
| 7) I feel comfortable with my role as a mother. | | | |

8) I understand my own needs.

9) I feel I have less patience than most mothers.

10) I am satisfied with my own ability to make good decisions about my children.

11) My family's needs are more important than my own.

12) I do not know where to look for resources to help me with my problems.

13) When it comes to my own children, I am an expert.

14) I encourage my husband to become involved with the care of our children.

15) I usually follow the advice of childrearing experts, even when their views differ from my own.

16) Few parents have to face the problems I face with my children.

17) I feel that as a mother, I am responsible for the happiness of my children.

18) It is a rare parent who can be even-tempered with children all day.

19) I feel good about my ability to make decisions about my life.

20) I cannot think of anybody else who can do a better job with my child than I can.

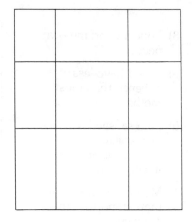

This "Mother's Attitude Inventory" was designed to check your feelings, not your efficiency. Its purpose is self-awareness. (The results of this test will not go into your permanent record.) Tests are indicators, not determiners. Accurate test results give a clue; it is up to us to solve the mystery.

Furthermore, your score will be affected by the kind of day you have had, the current ages and stages of your children, how much sleep you got last night, and how honestly you answered the questions.

To score your results, give yourself five points for each of the following responses:

Agree—2, 3, 5, 6, 7, 8, 10, 13, 14, 18, 19, 20;

Disagree—1, 4, 9, 11, 12, 15, 16, 17.

What does your score mean?

85-100 Hello, Supermom! You get an "A" in attitude. You are confident and comfortable in your role as mother.

65-80 Congratulations. You have a strongly positive

outlook on being a mother. You may have self-doubts occasionally but, then, what professional doesn't?

45-60 Your attitude about motherhood can best be described as neutral. Sometimes you act with strength and determination, other times you hesitate and worry. If you concentrate on those pluses, motherhood could become more enjoyable.

25-40 The kids seem to be doing fine here, but Mom is having problems. Pamper yourself a little.

0-20 This score indicates the least favorable attitude toward motherhood. But now the good news—there are many ways to feel better about yourself! Read on.

## Struggling for Self-Esteem

Whatever our score on this test, we are all sometimes disappointed in ourselves as mothers. Of course we all have those days regardless of our profession, days when we are less content with our performance than usual. It happens to airline pilots, it happens to computer programmers, it happens to bricklayers—but it happens to mothers more often.

Because of a mother's nurturing role, women are subject to problems and pressures that men seldom feel, most of which center around low self-esteem. When we make the change from non-mother to mother, we assume new legal and economic dependence on others. Becoming dependent often results in low aspirations and low esteem.

There are several forces regularly at work undermining a mother's self-confidence. The first is the confusion between *domestic* skills and *mothering* skills.

They are not the same. The fact that our society assumes they are is a major source of conflict and guilt for mothers. That confusion is what makes us feel we have failed as mothers when toys are everywhere and dinner is late, even though our children are healthy, independent and progressing well.

Domestic skills must somehow be provided in any household. A minimum level of nourishment and cleanliness is essential to human welfare at any age. Someone has to prepare the meals, sweep the floor, do the laundry. Levels of excellence beyond the minimal, however, are matters of talent and *choice*.

As one experienced mother put it, "There is a difference between Wonder Bread and a homemade loaf, but the difference has little to do with whether a child flourishes or withers. In truth, homemade bread broken in bitterness and quarreling contributes less to a child's overall growth than the tasteless, preservative-laden commercial product."

Mothering skills, on the other hand, are those which contribute to a child's total human growth and nurture a loving, confident, independent person. They are much more important than domestic skills and, for the most part, are independent of them. Mothering skills are what measure our effectiveness as parents. These skills involve listening, affirming and providing affection and encouragement, discipline and whatever else it takes to insure the emotional and physical development of our children.

It is vital that women separate their role as mother from their role as homemaker and accept themselves as they are. It is time we take pride in our strengths and stop feeling guilty about our inadequacies.

The second factor at work against our self-concept springs from the first: the attitude that there is a certain type of person ideally suited for motherhood (the "Earth Mother") and that the rest of us should reshape our personality accordingly. This "Right-Way-to-Mother" stereotype might be described as a bread-baking Girl Scout leader who is a good sport as well as a P.T.A. officer. She is soft-spoken, has infinite patience and is never at a loss for a new game or fascinating story when her preschooler needs one.

Yes, Virginia, there really may be women like that (there really may be a Santa Claus, too)! Some people do have a talent for dealing with babies and young children and prefer domestic challenges to any others.

Where does that leave other mothers who feel more creative in endeavors outside the home and who forgot the ending to "The Three Little Pigs" long ago? With a lot of guilt, especially in their children's preschool years.

The mothering skills involved in raising a small child—feeding, rocking, soothing, changing diapers, playing with a baby—come more easily to some than others. That does not mean, however, that those of us who have more adjusting to do are lesser mothers. It does mean we have different contributions to make— and more pain to endure in the early years of parenthood when "this-very-moment" demands run high. The constant pressures of infant and preschool days do gradually ease when children are in school with their own interests for part of the day. But when three-year-old Elizabeth wants to hear "Cinderella" for the fourth time and Mom wants to work on her doctoral thesis, grade school seems light years away.

One young mother, Nancy Dornsife, tells her side of the story:

> Some of my friends love the home life. Though at times they find motherhood frustrating, as we all

41

do, they can find their answers within the boundaries of the flower beds or the laundry. I admire and salute them, but I can't be like them. I have honestly tried, but it's just not me....

I don't think there is a formula for being a mother—homemade bread and chicken soup and always being home. I think motherhood expresses itself (or should) a little differently in all of us. If we each live for ourselves—for our happiness and our enrichment—we will be the best possible mothers because we will be fulfilled human beings. I would like to believe that years from now my children will remember, not that I was always there when they came home from school, but that I loved Robert Frost, Canada geese and lasagna.

The third problem mothers face is the experts—that faceless mass of professionals who stand looking over our shoulder, breathing down our neck, "killing us softly with their song."

Elaine Heffner, senior teaching associate in psychiatry at Cornell University Medical College says, "Childrearing information is always child-focused. That is, it is focused on educating mothers about a child's needs. Implicit in that material, however, is the judgment that only the needs of the child count."

And the needs of children as spelled out by the experts are often so great it is doubtful that any one person could possibly meet them all. American mothers suffer from what has been called a national parental inferiority complex. And many of the specialists who led us to this dilemma are beginning to realize their own part in it.

Doctor Benjamin Spock wrote recently, "Inability to be firm is...the commonest problem of parents in America today." And he blames this parental ineffectiveness on

...the child psychiatrists, psychologists, teachers, social workers, and pediatricians like myself.

In the 20th century parents have been persuaded that [these are] the only persons who know for sure how children should be managed....

This is a cruel deprivation that we professionals have imposed on mothers and fathers. Of course we did it with the best intentions....We didn't realize, until it was too late, how our know-it-all attitude was undermining the self-assurance of parents.

It is vital for mothers and fathers to understand that there is no one "right way" to parent. Rather, there is *our* way. The impact of parenthood is not that of isolated decisions which are right or wrong, but rather the long-term ability to respond to our child's individual needs.

Of course it would be foolish to disregard the valuable insights childhood researchers have made available in the last 60 years. We should consider that information just as any professional would. But we should not allow those opinions (and they are opinions) to intimidate us. We have spent years observing our own child and have personally guided her development. These are powerful credentials. When it comes to our children, we are the experts.

## O.K. Mothering

By the time we become mothers most of us have moved from dependence to independence to interdependence. The children we once were have matured and we now take care of ourselves. Even further, we have assumed responsibility for and with others. That makes us *winners*—not in the sense that we got there first or have made someone else lose, but rather in the sense that we have responded in a genuine way to our own needs and the needs of those around us.

People who do not make that adjustment are *losers* (according to James and Jongeward in their book *Born to Win*). Losers rarely live life in the present. They completely miss now by looking back on what has been, or looking forward to what will be.

Losers lament, "If only...": "...I had waited to have a child"; "...I had two children instead of three"; "...my husband were different."

Losers say, "How wonderful life will be when...": "...the baby is potty-trained"; "...the children are all in school"; "...I learn to stop screaming."

Transactional Analysis (TA) is one method of overcoming the moments in our lives when we act more like losers than winners. TA's goal is to help a person say, "I'm O.K. and you're O.K." Our goal is "O.K. Mothering."

O.K. Mothering begins by allowing others to give us support. We all need to feel good about ourselves, and positive strokes help us feel that way. James and Jongeward describe positive strokes as "...a look, a word, or any act that says, 'I know you're there.'" In many cases we may actually have implicit rules that keep us from getting the positive kinds of attention we need. Here are some examples of rules which say, "I'm not O.K.":

1) A mother's job is never done. (No matter how much we do we dwell on what we haven't done.)

2) A mother should *never* _____ (hit a child, use profanity...You fill in the blank).

3) Always be humble. Never pat yourself on the back or accept a compliment.

4) It's not nice to ask. People who love you should know what you need.

5) Always say yes. It's not nice to say no.

6) Affectionate expression is appropriate only in private.

We will receive more positive strokes and feel better about ourselves if we change these rules. It will help our children if they incorporate these new attitudes too. Here are the rules that say, "I'm O.K.":

1) It's O.K. to look on the bright side, to think of what you have done rather than what you have not.

2) It's O.K. to make mistakes. We are all human and fall short of perfection.

3) It's O.K. to be honest and pat ourselves on the back. It's also O.K. to take a compliment.

4) It's O.K. to ask for what we want.

5) It's O.K. to say no when we mean it.

6) Warm and affectionate feelings are O.K. any time and any place.

Now doesn't that feel better?

Life is full of conflicts. But we make it a no-lose situation when we can accept ourselves as we are and still challenge ourselves to become all that we can be— understanding and affirming our individual gifts and limits as God's work. The process is called growing up, and it is something we spend our whole lives doing.

A newborn child needs an adult for guidance, protection, socialization. Parents have that responsibility, and there are fringe benefits. Here is how some women have described their own growth since becoming mothers:

—"Since becoming a mother I'm much more flexible. I've learned how to handle it when life throws me a curve. I've learned that it's not absolutely necessary to know what's going to happen next."

—"I'm much less concerned about what others expect of me now that I've become a mother, and much more concerned about what I expect of myself."

—"Since becoming a mother I've stopped blaming other people for my mistakes. I've learned to make decisions and take the consequences of those decisions—good and bad."

—"To me the whole point of motherhood is growth, but I still sometimes find myself fighting it. I think, 'This is too hard. It's too tough to be so important to a small child.'"

New attitudes are a sure sign of growth. Measuring our own growth involves understanding the parts of ourselves which are one-dimensional and the parts which have expanded.

### Dealing With Failure

But no matter how much growing a mother does, there is no escaping failure of some kind. Even a winner must learn to lose with style.

What about those mistakes, disasters and failures that we all regularly face? Some endeavors are odds-on for failure—like entering the Pillsbury Bake-Off or trying to toilet-train the baby in one day. You assume you will lose. This is more fate than a personality flaw, so we do not punish ourselves.

What is difficult are unexpected failures in situations which are normally no-risk. You and your husband argue when everything is going well. Your child who has been an "A"-student is having trouble in school. You spend hours preparing a special meal for your family and someone says, "Yuch! I'm not gonna eat that stuff." Your 20-month-old, who has slept through the night since he was six weeks old, doesn't anymore. Those are the failures that weigh you down.

Our failures are as unique as we are. They give us solid information about ourselves even if it is hard to hear. If we look at our failures carefully, they too can become positive factors in our life.

Make a list of any disappointments that have come your way in the last six months. Then look for a pattern. While any single calamity may have lots of explanations, several seen together show a tendency which can be recognized and corrected.

Are your failures in the "always late" category? Some of us seem to rush through life. As one mother explained, "I usually begin sentences with either 'Hurry up!' or 'Quick!' Then I add, 'You can tie your shoe (or finish your cookie, or read your book) on the way.'"

Some of us find it difficult to delegate authority, needing to feel in control of every situation. "It's just easier to do it myself," says the mother of three boys. "If I don't do it myself, it's never done to my satisfaction."

We may have a pattern of being impatient and quick-tempered. We may be undependable or have trouble keeping a secret. But whatever our failure patterns, the first step is to recognize that those problems exist and then do something about them.

Probably one of the most common human failures is a fear of looking at our own mistakes. If we can think of nothing in our lives which would rate an "F," perhaps we have avoided mistakes by being over-careful. We may be so afraid to fail that we choose small, safe goals at the cost of avoiding something new, challenging and ultimately satisfying.

One thing for sure, your failures are just as much a part of you as your successes. And it helps to remember that failure may eventually lead to progress. The only real failure is the one from which we learn nothing.

Imagine what a total failure Calvary must have seemed to Christ's followers at the time. But in the light of Easter, no believer can ever say that any failure is total and irrevocable. Throughout life we often experience a kind of dying to ourselves so that we can be born to a new depth of living.

So when you are down and out, trying to teach the baby to eat with a spoon for the 150th time, remember this: Woody Allen flunked motion picture production at New York University. Barbara Jordan, U.S. representative from Texas, was defeated in an election for president of her freshman college class. Leon Uris failed high school English three times.

Failures are a part of life. They are not declarations of personal worth. Everyone fails—even our children.

## Our Child and Failure

As mothers, we see our children as an extension of ourselves. So at times we see their failures as our own. Psychologists say that seeing our children as "us" is a normal developmental step in the parent-child relationship, part of the bonding process. In early parenthood we may look to our children to confirm our virtues and prove our basic lovableness. We *must* be someone special—just look at this remarkable child we have produced! Warm feelings flow in toward ourselves and out toward the baby. But if the baby isn't special, is there something wrong with us?

Psychiatrist Aaron Stern says that some years ago when he told parents, "You have a nice, average, normal youngster," the mother and father would be thrilled. But today, he says, when he tells parents, "You have a nice, average, normal youngster," they are depressed.

Although it may be common for new parents to have difficulty accepting limitations in their child, it is vital that we overcome those feelings as our child grows. The idea that our child's failures are ours is one we must soon relinquish so that the child can make mistakes and still believe he or she is O.K. If we see our children's faults as our own, how can we ever allow them to fail—and learn?

Children must be permitted to fail because, in Stern's words, "You are not going to get anywhere unless you are free to fail." He says childhood offers a marvelous opportunity to fail because, "In childhood it's not expensive to fail."

Speaking on Phil Donahue's show, Stern gave the following example: "Your child may have to pick a course in high school; maybe he takes the wrong math course, maybe it's trigonometry instead of geometry. The worst thing that'll happen is that he has to go to summer school.... But no, we do the research, we meet the guidance counselor, we go through all the colleges he might get into, we worry about the SAT's...in any event what we're doing is we're constantly intruding on his ability to earn his self-esteem and not respecting him as a person who can fail as well as succeed."

Sometimes we expect our children to achieve what we didn't in our own lives. We want them to be all the things we need them to be. But that isn't good either for us or for them.

In spite of what we would like to do, we cannot give our children self-esteem. Self-esteem is something that must be earned and developed; it takes effort, vulnerability and bruising. But if we permit our children the right to fail and to learn from their failures, we permit them the right to their own adulthood.

## Action Steps for a Healthy Self-Concept

Physician-columnist Walter Menninger says, "Our children, being our creation, are to some degree a living part of us—an extension of us. Our feelings toward them will, then, reflect some of our feelings toward ourselves. If we have self-doubts, or a 'bad' sense of ourself, we are likely to assume that our child is similarly bad and perceive our child that way."

The children suffer from adult self-doubt. Child abuse in this country has reached epidemic proportions. Dr. Elaine Billmire, a pediatrician at Children's Hospital Medical Center in Cincinnati, explains that the typical child abuser is not a psychotic monster. Rather such a person is unhappy, poor at controlling his or her feelings, and is under a great deal of stress.

Our own feeling of well-being, then, is vital to the well-being of those around us. Loss of self-esteem occurs when there is a difference between the mother we think we ought to be and the mother we think we are. Note the emphasis on the word *think*. Reality is irrelevant here. We can be the best mother on planet Earth, but unless we *know* it, the fact has no effect on our self-image.

For everyone's sake, take some steps toward improving your self-esteem:

1) *Set your own standards.* So your mother-in-law who expects a sparkling house and well-groomed kids is coming over. Don't panic! You could bathe the kids and clean like mad—but you'll only end up resenting her intrusion on your day. Consider your own needs instead. Prepare for her arrival to your satisfaction, welcome her warmly and refuse to worry about what she may be thinking. You might even find yourself enjoying your time with her.

2) *Revise your standards to realistic proportions.* The Serene Madonna exists only in Renaissance portraits. Real mothers—all of us—have difficult days; we aren't always patient and in control. There is no law that says we don't have the right to show our feelings if they are reasonable. There are times when parents need

to react as Jesus did in the Temple: with justifiable anger.

3) *Maximize your successes.* Forget the myths discussed in Chapter 1. Mothers do *not* always feel good, look nice, have clean houses, even tempers and a sense of fulfillment. You don't really want to scrub the floor in high heels, anyway, and your children aren't ever going to be perfect. Neither are you. But you are good! Next time you feel awful because you lost patience and yelled at the kids, remind yourself of the many times you said and did exactly the right thing.

4) *Build in your own rewards.* Mothers perform in isolated surroundings; they get no feedback. No one sees most of your really fine performances with the kids and the housework. No one is going to deliver a pat on the back—unless you do. Read a novel instead of cleaning the sink while the baby naps; watch *Donahue* instead of washing windows. Call a friend and waste a happy half hour with her. And don't feel guilty. You work hard and you deserve a reward.

5) *Bloom where you're planted—and repot yourself when necessary.* Admit to yourself that life is hard and sometimes unfair. It will rain on the day the baby has a bad cold, you have a headache and the must-do list has no end. The washer is sure to break down when the budget is at its lowest ebb. And it is not your fault. Break away from it like this mother:

> Last winter my children were two and four. I had no car and wasn't able to get involved in much, but I knew I needed a change. One afternoon I went to a home for the elderly which was just a block from my house. I walked in with these two little kids and said, "Here we are! Is there anything we can do?"
> 
> We've been visiting some new "grandmas" and

"grandpas" once or twice a month ever since. It helps the people we've come to know and love, and it helps us.

Self-esteem *can* be found in mothering. But we must examine our role in relation to our humanity, coming to terms with our accomplishments as well as our failures. We must realize that our children are people, but so is their mother. It is only when we learn to understand ourselves that we will learn to understand our children, only when we learn to respect ourselves that we can teach our children that same respect. Then we are free to live life fully as a parent *and* as a person.

## For Discussion and Awareness

1) Do you feel embarassed when your child misbehaves in public? How do you handle your feelings about this misbehavior?

2) Which stage of your child's (children's) development has been the most pleasant for you? The most unpleasant?

3) Have you read many child-care books? Have they helped you? Have any child-care books worked to undermine your self-confidence?

4) In what ways are you an "O.K. parent"? What are some things you really feel good about as a parent?

5) Can you think of a time when you allowed your child to fail—and learn from that failure?

6) In what ways have you matured since becoming a mother?

## Idea for Action

With the help of a friend, think of a failure pattern which seems to recur in your life and determine a plan of action to turn that failure into success.

## Bibliography

Dornsife, Nancy L. "I'm My Kind of Mother." *Redbook* (May, 1975), pp. 35-40.

Heffner, Elaine. *Mothering*. New York: Doubleday, 1978.

James, Muriel, and Dorothy Jongeward. *Born to Win*. Reading, Massachusetts: Addison-Wesley Co., 1971.

Morrone, Wenda Wardell. "Failures—They Have to Be Worth Something." *Glamor* (October, 1976), pp. 80-83.

Spock, Benjamin, M.D. "How Not to Bring Up a Bratty Child." *Redbook* (February, 1974), pp. 29-31.

Viorst, Judith. *It's Hard to Be Hip Over Thirty and Other Tragedies of Married Life*. Cleveland, Ohio: World Publishing, 1969.

The life I have chosen as wife and mother entrains a whole caravan of complications.... It involves food and shelter; meals, planning, marketing, bills, and making ends meet in a thousand ways. It involves not only the butcher, the baker, the candlestick maker but countless other experts to keep my modern house with its modern "simplifications" functioning properly....

This is not the life of simplicity, but the life of multiplicity that the wise men warn us of.

—**Anne Morrow Lindbergh**
*A Gift From the Sea*

# Chapter 4
# Mothering and Management

Mothers are managers. The baby has the chicken pox, Dad has the flu, the dog has diarrhea—but somehow we manage.

One of the reasons motherhood can seem overwhelming is that it offers so many possibilities. We are challenged to love in the most unselfish way. Minds and characters are ours to shape and guide. We hold the possibility of creating a truly comfortable home, nourishing others with food and warmth. We can become professional outside as well as inside the home, offer help to those who need it, and do whatever it takes to become a whole person in every sense of the word.

As mothers we are free to do that. We are also free to climb Mt. Kilimanjaro, walk the Appalachian Trail and swim the English Channel—but we don't *have* to do it all, at least not this week. The easy way out is to don our "Supermom" suit and fly in spite of the odds. But that is impractical and, besides, we want to live to see our grandchildren.

A much better approach is to learn to evaluate our priorities and manage our activities so that we do not spend our entire life simply "pleasing people." Not long ago the speaker at a retreat reminded those attending that reading and studying about management is a "very Christian" thing to do. He said that the more skilled we are at administering life, the richer our experiences will become and the more we can free ourselves to be with others.

### Management Techniques

Managers, like mothers, are not born but made. Some of the qualities which make us outstanding mothers make us outstanding managers as well. Robert Bidwell, a management consultant for many years, has listed basic maxims for excellence in management. We can easily apply them to our own job description:

1) *Find out what your boss wants done.* Since in most cases we have met the boss and she is us, good mothering is a matter of defining our own objectives, goals and priorities. Of course it is vital to talk frequently with your husband and insist on two-way communication.

2) *Manage your frustrations.* Yes, this is a tough

one. But the golden rule of any supervisory position applies here—don't complain to your subordinates. It's self-defeating.

3) *Power comes from below.* Your people will make you successful—eventually. For Mom this success comes and goes with the stages of growth her child experiences, but the fact remains that our children are excellent resources and we should use them well.

4) *Don't waste your time trying to make people happy.* Happiness comes from within. As Abraham Lincoln said long ago, "Most people are about as happy as they make up their minds to be." But happiness is contagious, and children react to a smile more quickly than anyone.

5) *Be firm, fair and consistent.* Consistency is next to godliness in motherhood. Keep your rules to an absolute minimum, then make sure those rules are respected.

When it comes to firmness, try to have all the facts. But don't be afraid to say "I'm sorry" if new facts prove you wrong. For a mother to admit she is wrong is probably one of the best ways to teach her children one of life's hardest lessons.

6) *Do it now.* This is Parkinson's law, and most mothers know if they don't do it now, they will only have to do it later. Remember Parkinson's second law as well: "Delay is the deadliest form of self-denial."

7) *Keep your word.* You *did* say that you would take the children to the swimming pool when the baby woke up from her nap. Make few commitments, but once you have made them, move heaven and earth to keep your word. After all, how can we expect our children to tell the truth if we don't?

8) *Listen.* Someone said, "A parent is a person who listens and listens until she can't listen any more, then

she keeps right on listening." Good managers take time to listen to what is being said to them, especially by subordinates.

The secret of getting people ("little" people as well as "big" ones) to do what we want, Bidwell explains, is to explain the task, then ask them to repeat that explanation. You will be amazed at what they thought you said. Don't be surprised or hurt when the message comes back wrong. Few adults can repeat such directions.

9) *Remember, people don't make mistakes on purpose.* When your child makes a mistake in front of you, thank him for the opportunity he has given you to show him how to do it the right way. Our children's mistakes are a valuable teaching tool.

Remember, too, that the manager who is working toward personal growth thinks not only of the child's error, but asks herself what she did wrong the last time she was confronted by a cup of spilled milk.

10) *Lead by example.* Ames and Chase say it best in *Don't Push Your Preschooler:* "You teach your child by what you say, you teach your child by what you do, you teach your child by what you are." If you want your child to be polite, you must be polite. If you want your children to respect you, you must respect them and yourself.

Besides applying these basis management techniques, an effective manager works to achieve three major goals:

1) She clears her life of negative emotions.
2) She manages her own needs.
3) She becomes an efficient decision-maker.

## Clearing Away Negative Emotions
Self-esteem has been defined as the ability and skill

to manage one's own environment. People who have high esteem make things happen. But self-esteem is not something we "get" and then have forever. It must be exercised or we loose it.

Basic blocks to self-esteem include those negative emotions we have all felt at times: anger, guilt, shame, anxiety, depression and worry.

*Anger* is generated when a person feels helpless in a situation. Our child doesn't obey. Our lives are disorganized. Our esteem is jeopardized. We feel anger.

*Guilt* results from the transgression of a standard or rule: "A mother should never scream at her child" or "A mother should never lose patience." A mother has to be careful about saying "never." When standards are unrealistic, guilt can become a constant companion.

*Shame* results from not completing a task or reaching an objective. We have not folded the laundry and no one can find clean underwear. We have not gone to the grocery and the baby is out of formula. We are trying our best but, somehow, that is not good enough.

Some people work to avoid shame at any cost. They think, "Why try? I know I'll never do it right." And so potential remains unfulfilled—even if ego is intact.

*Anxiety* is a nervous feeling in the pit of our stomach. It comes from not knowing who we are in a situation. We have had a baby. We are a mother. But what does that mean? Unless we can distinguish our own individuality from the role we have assumed, we may live our whole lives, as Thoreau said, "in quiet desperation."

Depression comes when we reach the depths of anxiety, when all these negative emotions become knotted together. In most cases we deal with depression by avoiding life, by becoming apathetic, withdrawn. A mother who lets her children sit in front of the television all day because she "can't cope" is struggling for her own emotional survival.

A child forces us into being loving and directed toward another. If handled properly, these experiences can dramatically promote our growth. If handled improperly, our lives can become days of endless anxiety. We turn into worriers.

## Dealing With Worry

Worry is the worst possible waste of a manager's time. It wipes out today with concern about yesterday or tomorrow. Worrying can easily be distinguished from problem-solving: Problem-solving leads to action; worry leads to nothing.

Our society encourages worry, reports Wayne Dyer, Ph.D.:

> You prove your love by doing an appropriate amount of worrying at the correct time. ("Of course I'm worried, it's only natural when you care about someone.") But not one moment of worry will make things any better. In fact worry will very likely make you less effective in dealing with the present. And worry has nothing to do with love in a relationship in which each person has the right to be what he chooses without any unreasonable conditions imposed by the other.

Typical worries of motherhood might include: Will I have a healthy baby? Can I go through with natural childbirth? Will I be able to breastfeed? Is she gaining fast enough? Is he gaining too fast? Is she as smart as the baby next door? (Nobody ever admits to this one.) Will he go to kindergarten wearing diapers, sucking on his pacifier, still carrying his "blankie"? Will I ever not be tired? Will I be able to communicate my values to my child? Will my children like themselves and be self-confident adults? Will they choose friends wisely? Will they be able to function well and find fulfillment in life?

There are alternatives to such worries. According to Dyer, we should view today as a time to live by recognizing the absurdity of worry. We should ask ourselves, "Has anything ever changed as a result of my worrying about it?"

A more productive approach is to take the time and energy we use worrying and turn it into action. If you are worried about having a healthy baby, find out what a developing child needs (good nourishment, vitamins, etc.) and doesn't need (any kind of drugs, exposure to certain illnesses and so on). Once a pregnant woman understands that she has some control over the health of her baby, she can concentrate on providing those things to the best of her ability.

If you're considering natural childbirth or breastfeeding (and hurray for you if you are), take advantage of the many excellent classes available everywhere on both, then discuss specifics with your doctor. The same kind of information is available to help you determine your child's developmental progress.

As for more cosmic worries like our ability to communicate values and our child's fulfillment in life, we must remember that we influence our children through sensible guidance and the example we offer in our own lives. Open dialogue with our children from the time they are small is essential too. Then when our children are older and face major decisions, we will be the first people they turn to—because they can talk to us.

Of course, as we have said before, life is not predictable: That is the beauty and pain of it. But even in the face of uncertainty we can turn worry to action through prayer. No matter how devastating a problem may seem, it becomes manageable if we remember that "...nothing is impossible with God" (Luke 1:37).

In short, don't let worry rule your life and waste your energy. Consider worry a caution light flashing on and off in your head and think, "This is an area of concern for me. How can I resolve it?"

Then do your homework. Talk to others, read, look for answers which relieve your mind and point to a plan of action. Make your worries count for new knowledge and new confidence in important areas of personal concern.

## Managing Needs

Psychologist A.H. Maslow says we can understand a person's actions as attempts to satisfy unsatisfied needs. Those levels of need include:

1) physiological needs (survival, basic functions to support life);
2) safety needs (security, dependency, need for order, structure, law);
3) love needs (tenderness, affection, mutual concern);
4) esteem needs (respect from self and others based on development toward maturity);
5) self-actualization needs (discovery of self and one's own potential).

We are motivated, according to Maslow, by each level of need—*in order*—until it is satisfied. If a mother has not slept in 24 hours, she will be primarily motivated by her need for sleep (physiological need). Higher levels of need (love, esteem) become unimportant. After she has rested she can move from the physical to other levels.

A mother can get stuck on safety needs when she so fears losing her secure if stifling routine that she clings to rules others have told her will work: "A mother should be there when her child gets home from school" or "If a mother doesn't work she's uninteresting." Such rules cause guilt and shame when she doesn't follow them; anger when she does. All of this results in constant anxiety and eventual depression which leaves her immobilized and incapable of growth.

People—children and parents—have needs. The following is a random sample of needs (in no particular order) that mothers listed for themselves and for their children.

| *Mother's Needs* | *Child's Needs* |
| --- | --- |
| time to myself | time to himself or herself |
| recreation and play | recreation and play |
| nourishment, cleanliness, rest | nourishment, cleanliness, rest |
| love and hugs | love and hugs |
| intellectual stimulation | intellectual stimulation |
| attention and pampering | attention and pampering |
| encouragement | encouragement |
| freedom | freedom |
| praise | praise |
| family | family |
| home | home |
| friends | friends |
| adult contact | adult contact |
| appreciation | appreciation |
| understanding | understanding |
| discipline | discipline |
| respect | respect |
| communication | communication |
| kindness | kindness |
| guidance | guidance |
| good example | good example |

The mothers who originally listed these needs did not come up with these two identical lists. At first they called a mother's need for personal care "grooming" and a child's "cleanliness." They called a mother's need for entertainment "recreation" and the child's "play." It was only after putting the lists together that it became obvious: "Hey, we have the very same needs as our children. Maybe in different quantities—but not much different."

Children and adults have similar needs, and both sets of needs must be met if we are to achieve maximum success and happiness for everyone concerned.

Mothers manage needs—their own and their child's. Those needs are mismanaged if the child's demands become so constant and overwhelming that a mother loses all sense of herself. If we only react to our child, with never a thought of our own needs, we will eventually reach the breaking point. We will lose the balance between self and others. Conversely, if we only react to ourself, with never a thought to our child's needs, our child will suffer greatly. The balance is crucial.

Psychologists say the mature individual balances needs with a low degree of conflict. And yet a certain amount of this conflict is common to every human being. Maslow emphasizes that it takes years of discipline and development to approach true self-actualization where such understanding is a matter of course.

Everyone needs to create her own personal space. A mother works toward self-esteem by making conscious decisions which result in the delicate and critical balance between how much she gives and how much she gets.

When we are managing needs, the skill of decision-making is vital. Effective managers make effective decisions.

## Becoming an Effective Decision-Maker

Life is filled with decisions: pecan pie or strawberries and cream, Mozart or Manilow, two children or three. And the more experienced we become at life, the greater our options. Over the years we move from a choice of goods to a selection of greats. The variety is limitless—and often sheer misery.

Decisions are difficult because they seldom involve a clear choice between right and wrong but often a choice between *almost* right and *possible* wrong, or among good, better and best.

Institutional consultant David Ruhmkorff says that good decisions come only through the development of alternatives. He has described decision-making as a circular problem-solving process which involves four steps. Its roadmap looks like this:

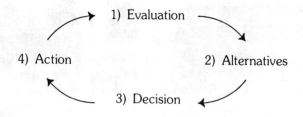

1) Evaluation

4) Action

2) Alternatives

3) Decision

Notice that the decision itself is step three in the problem-solving process. Often we admonish ourselves, "I must make a decision about this!" Then we expect to make a Solomon-like judgment with neither evaluation nor an analysis of alternatives. The result is a bad decision or none at all.

What decisions do mothers have to make? As the manager of that highly specialized social unit, the family, we face literally dozens of decisions every day.

Some are so automatic we may not even be aware that we are making them. What time should we get up? Will we have ham and eggs or cold cereal for breakfast? When should the children leave for school? What should we do when the baby cries? Which toys do we buy for Christmas? Will we use Gerber baby food or make our own?

Besides those garden-variety decisions, mothers encounter many other decisions which are more complex: How much television and which programs should my children watch? Should my four-year-old go to a preschool? Which one? Should I return to work? When? Full- or part-time? Should my husband accept a promotion which could mean a move to another state? Should I go back to school?

The list of decisions we face is as long as life itself. In order to choose wisely it is important to understand that our values influence every decision we make. Evaluation, the first step in the decision-making process, allows us to study our present situation by gathering the facts which influence our everyday lives.

The following is an exercise in evaluation, that first critical step in problem-solving. Allow yourself two minutes to complete each of the following five sections.

## Exercise in Evaluation

1) In my life it would be valuable for me if:

a) _____

b) _____

c) _____

d) _____

e) _____

2) Those things in my life from which I derive the greatest pleasure are:

a) _____

b) _____

c) _____

d) _____

e) _____

3) The accomplishments in which I take the greatest pride are:

a) _____

b) _____

c) _____

d) _____

e) _____

4) I derive the greatest satisfaction from being a mother when:

a) _____

b) _____

c) _____

d) _____

e) _____

What does all of this mean? Find out by completing the next statement:

5) By doing this exercise, I have learned:

a) _____

b) _____

c) _____

d) _____

e) _____

Your answer to question five should give you insights into where you are and what problems (decisions) you face. The evaluation exercise is designed to point out resources, describe needs and show constraints in solving those problems.

For example, by doing this exercise one mother learned:

1) "I have a need to be with my children much of the time when they are young."
2) "I want to be with my husband and children as a family often."
3) "My career as a mother is of primary importance in my life."
4) "My most important accomplishments include my family, but they also include activities beyond that of wife and mother."

5) "I have the skills, training and ambition to pursue a career outside my home."

The exercise points out this mother's *resources* (her family and career goals, her skills, training, motivation). It describes her *needs* (the need for her family, her family's need for her, the need for fulfillment inside and outside the family). It shows her *constraints* (handling a full-time job as mother while accomplishing a professional career outside the home.)

Decisions are not cold and calculated. Behavior is attached to feelings. Through the information gained in evaluation we can determine how we feel about important issues. We can further analyze those feelings, as well as our resources and needs, by asking how our life-style affects the problem. Some questions we might ask include:

1) How much available time can I come up with?
2) What are my financial needs?
3) What are my responsibilities?
4) What family-life priorities I value affect other aspects of my life?

If I have learned from the evaluation exercise that I am interested in a career outside as well as inside the home, I need to know whether I want to work full-time or part-time and how the values I hold in mothering will mesh with my job responsibilities. In answering the life-style questions, one mother found:

1) "I have some available time because my children are in preschool. I also have trusted friends who will provide excellent care for my children when I need time."
2) "My husband can currently support our family on his salary alone, but we would benefit from extra income."
3) "I have serious responsibilities to see that my

own and my children's needs are met in the best way possible."

4) "Family-life priorities I value include:
   a) being with my children much of the time when they are young;
   b) having my children cared for in my absence by someone who is responsible and loving and who can provide a stimulating environment;
   c) being with my husband and children as a family as often as possible."

## Discovering Alternatives

After feelings, values, problems and resources are identified, it is time to consider the second step in decision-making: discovering alternatives.

Alternatives can be defined as opportunities, options, potentials—the meat of decision. When considering alternatives we should always move from our strengths: those things we pinpointed as resources during evaluation.

Discovering alternatives is a real detective game. We become investigators in search of people and ideas which suggest choices. To do this it is crucial that we go out to others. Very often we are locked into our own experiences and can personally see no alternatives.

If we have never gone back to work with young children at home, or picked out a nursery school for our child, or taken an afternoon for ourselves every week, it can be difficult to imagine how to do it. Often we need somebody else to offer a fresh point of view. It is usually much easier to be creative when you are on the outside of a problem looking in.

Having been there helps too. Ask another mother who has successfully gone back to work, or picked a preschool, or taken an afternoon for herself regularly *how* she did it. There are lots of resources out there—people, books and services which can greatly aid in our research. All it takes is determination to discover the possibilities.

Once you have come up with a list of alternatives, consider them in light of your values. For example, you want to work outside the home, but one of your values is that you be home with your children much of the time when they are young. That is a value which will influence your decision to return to work.

If you need to be with your children much of the time, you will probably want a part-time job so that you will have more flexible hours. However, if it is vital that you get a job for financial reasons, the money you need to earn may necessarily replace your desire to be home. Remember that there are no perfect alternatives. Every solution has its drawbacks.

One helpful way to decide between alternatives is to analyze them in relation to your values. A scoring grid like the one on page 73 allows you to quantify alternatives by giving each a number of points as it relates to your values. Score the alternatives on a scale of one (low) to 10 (high).

This sample shows how the mother who is considering work outside the home filled out her grid. If the mother works full-time regular hours she will have little time at home with her small children during the day, so she rated that alternative one point in relation to the value "mother home with children." Since regular full-time hours coincide with the father's work schedule, he could not be home with the children while the mother is gone, so she rated that value one point as well. Full-time work, however, would probably result in the best salary so she gave 10 points to the "financial contribution" category. The mother is not sure whether

# Decision concerning work outside the home

| VALUES | Mother home with children | Father home when mother works | Financial contribution | Family together on weekends | Mothering satisfaction vs. outside career goals | |
|---|---|---|---|---|---|---|
| **ALTERNATIVES** | | | | | | |
| Full-time work regular hours | 1 | 1 | 10 | 5 | 1 | 18 points |
| Full-time work flex-time | 4 | 4 | 10 | 5 | 6 | 29 points |
| Part-time work regular hours | 7 | 7 | 5 | 7 | 8 | 34 points |
| Part-time work flex-time | 8 | 8 | 5 | 8 | 9 | 38 points |
| Free-lance work at home | 9 | 9 | 4 | 10 | 10 | 42 points |
| No job outside the home | 10 | 10 | 1 | 10 | 1 | 32 points |

full-time work would mean free weekends or not, so she rated "family together on weekends" five points. And because a full-time job outside her home would go far to further the mother's professional career, but would work against her need to be with the children much of the time when they are young, she rated "balance of mothering satisfaction and outside career goals" one point.

The mother completed her entire grid in a similar fashion. After she added all scores and compared them, she found that free-lance work at home (with a score of 42) was probably the best choice for her at this particular time. The scores also indicated that the alternatives of flex-time part-time work (with a score of 38) and part-time work with regular hours (with a score of 34) were desirable and should be considered when the mother begins her job hunt and discovers which employment possibilities are available for her.

You can make a similar grid to score alternative solutions to any problem. The number of squares will vary with the range of alternatives and values you are weighing, but the design remains the same.

When you actually select the best alternative, remember that a decision is always a risk. No one ever solves a major problem without support.

Think in terms of your life-style and friendships, then ask yourself, "Who will support me in this decision? In whom do I confide? Which friends can I rely on?"

There is an important difference between friends and acquaintances. Friends do not judge, lay on guilt, or offer cheap advice. Acquaintances do.

Once you know which friends you will need to rely on in your decision, talk to them about it. Tell them, "I feel I need support to carry out this decision (working at home free-lance, having another child, beginning a weight-loss program). I want to know what kind of support I can expect from you."

You are up front. You have described your hopes. After their answer, you should be aware of your chances for success.

## Acting on Your Decision

After a decision is made, the only remaining step is action. Researchers say it is O.K. to make a decision and not act on it immediately. Very often we need time to make a decision happen. You can't necessarily start your part-time job tomorrow just because you made the decision today.

If you are not going to act immediately, it can be helpful to set a planning date for your decision right away. You can say something like, "On February 13, I will begin to plan my job-hunting strategy for free-lancing at home."

Once you have put your plan into action, you will have to go back to the drawing board of evaluation to make sure that the decision you have implemented really fits your life and your feelings. So we come full-circle in decision-making and the whole process begins again...and again...and again...

## Mother and Manager

Mother is the chief executive in charge of just about everything. Knowledge of the qualities that make a good manager are important, but are in themselves only techniques, not promises. We still must free ourselves from self-defeating emotions like anger, shame, guilt, anxiety, depression and worry.

There is, after all, no perfect style of leadership. One mother gets the job done with high drama, while another does it simply with a look. What characterizes the effective mother-manager is that unique ability to do the job well—her way.

## For Discussion and Awareness

1) Are you a good manager? How do you like being the boss of your own little corporation?

2) How successful are you at meeting your own needs as well as the needs of your children?

3) Is there a parenting situation in which you feel helpless and therefore angry? Could you avoid the anger (or depression or guilt) by accepting the fact that this is a situation over which you have little if any control?

4) Do you ever get depressed? How do you pull yourself out of that depression?

5) What are some worries you have as a mother? How can you deal with those worries constructively?

6) Are there any problems or decisions which you currently face in your life? Do you see any alternatives to your present situation?

## Idea for Action

Attend a workshop for managers. (Contact the Career Planning Office or the Continuing Education Department of a local college for information about such a workshop.)

## Bibliography

Ames, Louise Bates, Ph.D., and Joan Ames Chase, Ph.D. *Don't Push Your Preschooler*. New York: Harper and Row, 1974.

Bidwell, Robert. "Misery, Mayhem and Management." *The Cincinnati Enquirer Magazine* (January 4, 1976), pp. 20-23.

Dyer, Wayne, Ph.D. *Your Erroneous Zones*. New York: Funk and Wagnall, 1976.

Goble, Frank. *The Third Force*. New York: Grossman Publishers, 1970.

Lindbergh, Anne Morrow. *A Gift From the Sea*. New York: Pantheon, 1955.

Maltz, Maxwell, M.D. *Psycho-Cybernetics for Creative Living*. New York: Pocketbooks, 1977.

Maslow, Abraham. *Motivation and Personality*. New York: Harper and Row, 1954.

When I was young, Daddy was going to throw me up in the air and catch me and I would giggle until I couldn't giggle any more, but he had to change the furnace filter and there wasn't time.

When I was young, Mama was going to read me a story and I was going to turn the pages and pretend I could read, but she had to wax the bathroom and there wasn't time....

When I grew up and left home to be married, I was going to sit down with Mom and Dad and tell them I loved them and I would miss them. But Hank (he's my best man and a real clown) was honking the horn in front of the house, so there wasn't time.

—Erma Bombeck
*At Wit's End*

# Chapter 5
# Time: Taming It

Mothers are obsessed with time. We were pregnant for nine months. Our labor lasted seven hours, beginning with 15-second contractions, 20 minutes apart. The baby was born at 6:45, and now if it is not feeding time or bath time or playtime or story time, then it is bedtime.

But time is much more than the hours and minutes that tick it off. It is a matter of being aware of the present—the relationships that shape it and the energy we put into it.

Time is ours to use. It is a natural resource, supply unknown. If the question is, "How do I make the most of my lifetime?," the answer has to be, "By knowing what's important to me and what I want to do."

"We all have plenty of time to do everything we really *want* to do," says Alan Lakein, who has given his time management seminar to over 15,000 people and advised companies like IBM and Standard Oil on the best use of time.

The first question, says Lakein in his book *How to Get Control of Your Time and Your Life* is, "What is the best use of my time right now?" Most people, he says, do not think about life in terms of spare minutes which they can put to productive use.

The second consideration is, "To whom does my time belong?" A mother's time is not completely her own. Peter Drucker explains, "The executive's time tends to belong to everybody else....Everybody can move in on his (her) time, and everybody does."

Distinctions must be made about who owns this time. Is it the baby's time? The doctor's time? The butcher's time? The plumber's time? If it is, then accept it, but be sure that *your* time is coming. Build in a part of the day which is entirely your own.

Mothers, unlike other managers, don't have the luxury of telling their secretary, "Mother will not be accepting calls this afternoon," and putting the world on hold while she cleans up some long overdue paperwork or housework. But, mothers can steal minutes. We can practice switching on our "other-than-Mommy" mind at the exact moment Big Bird walks down Sesame Street, and do it with full knowledge that we may not complete the project in an hour, but we will make a dent in it.

What is unique about a mother's work is this: If she is doing it to specifications and all systems are normal, she will perform herself right out of a job in about 18 years.

A new person is much like any other project in its infancy. It consumes great amounts of time, to say nothing of blood, sweat and tears, to get it on its feet. Once on its feet, it needs constant supervision to make sure progress continues.

Once a child reaches the age of six, however, he has not only formed his basic personality and approximately 50 percent of his intellectual capacity, but he is reasonably independent as well. That stage of a child's growth marks a dramatic transition for the mother, too, because she is no longer needed all day, every day, once the child is in school. Similar changes occur as the child reaches teenage years and again when the young adult is ready for college or work. At that time a mother has to face the very real question, "What's next?"

## Looking Ahead

One excellent use of a mother's time is to ask "What's next?" long before her child's 18th birthday. We can do that by using our time now to think about the direction of our life.

Time-management experts emphasize the necessity of writing down goals. The advantage of writing goals on paper is that we are *forced* to plan. It puts our life in black and white, turning dreams into objectives.

### Goal-Planning Exercise

To plan goals most efficiently you will need a large pad of paper (legal size is good), a pencil and a friend (it helps to share ideas with someone else). Using a clean sheet for each question, write down as many answers as possible to these questions:

1) *What are your goals during your child's preschool years?*
   (Give yourself three minutes to make a list of everything that matters to you, from potty-training your two-year-old to reading *Newsweek* from cover to cover. Include your career, financial, social, personal and spiritual expectations. Try to fill the whole sheet.)

2) *What are your goals during your child's elementary and high school years?*
   (Again, give yourself three minutes to list what is important to you during this time—that your child be accepted at an Ivy League College, that you be accepted at an Ivy League College; that your daughter make the Olympic trials, that you make the Olympic trials; that your children become fulfilled human beings, that you become a fulfilled human being. Include financial, spiritual, personal and social goals.)

3) *Describe a day in your life as you hope it will be after your children are grown and have left home.*

After completing these three questions, compare them to see if they are compatible. Do you hope for a career when your children are older? If so, have you built those interests into your children's earlier years? If your perfect day includes calls from your daughter the doctor and your son the lawyer, you will need to ask if your mothering techniques are fostering such ambitions and if you will be financially ready to handle them.

Brainstorm as you reconsider your goals. Give yourself additional time to go back and clarify ideas. No one will hold you to what you write down, and your own wildest ideas may indicate some very real possibilities.

Once you are satisfied with your list of goals, the next step is to rate everything either "A," "B," or "C," according to priority. "A" marks the highest values— things like finishing your college education, seeing that little Meg learns addition and subtraction, taking in a foster child or cutting up your credit card so you will stop over-spending your budget.

Your "B" list should be of medium value and your "C's" low priorities like scrubbing the rafters in the attic. Give your first consideration to "A's" and your last to "C's." In fact you may find that "C's" don't really need to be done at all; not doing them will give you more time for what is important.

The basic issue in planning your life and your time is to decide what you really want—and then to take steps that will bring you closer to happiness.

Do you yearn for simplicity but live a life complicated by dance lessons, Cub Scouts and soccer practice? The answer is not necessarily to eliminate all outside activities, especially if such activity is part of your goals. But it could involve streamlining that activity. It could be as simple as organizing a car pool, or limiting your children's activities to two nights a week instead of four.

Part of our goal as parents is to help our child become an independent person, a confident adult. We are committed to a shared life with our family, but there are still choices to be made. It is possible to offer support to our children's activities without taking part in all of them. No mother who hates sports should have to sit through every Little League game. And children deserve the freedom to explore interests that are alien to their parents.

Here are three guidelines to help you spend your time wisely:

1) Do some things with your child just for her.
2) Do some things with your child for both of you.
3) Reserve some time to do your own thing.

## Efficiency

Even though we have set our priorities, there is still the matter of making most efficient use of time. Alan Lakein says that mothers have special problems with time because our hours are longer and we work harder than most executives. He also says we have fewer people available with whom to check reality. So now that we have made that list of goals, we should act on it immediately, whether the family room is vacuumed or not. Here is a crash course in making it happen:

1) *Find out what is happening to your time.* Keep a log for at least a week, writing down everything you do. Include shopping trips, phone calls, laundry, fixing meals, outside work, playing with the children, and so on. Once you see how you are spending your time, you can decide which of those things are most important ("A" priorities). Think of ways to delegate the less important tasks to other people (who may do them even better) or to eliminate the task altogether.

2) *Have a plan.* Make a list; then, don't lose the list. Again, number tasks in order of priority, and do them in that order. Include things that you want (not just *have*) to do. Remember the value of your time—that cash figure mentioned in Chapter 1. As a valuable employee you are entitled to days off, time to upgrade skills, meetings with peers and so on.

Make a new schedule every day, preferably at night

84

before you go to bed. Everything is calm then and you can better collect your thoughts. It also helps to check off items during the day as you complete them. The check marks are written proof of your accomplishments.

3) *Have a notebook.* Keep your lists in it. It should be small enough to accompany you everywhere. One page might contain the day's priorities, another the weekly shopping list, another the times of piano lessons, a new recipe from a neighbor, or notes about the project you have just begun.

4) *Schedule time slots.* Allow yourself 10 minutes to clean the bathroom, one hour to dust, 15 minutes to scrub the floor. Housework has a way of expanding to fill the time allowed for it. If something of a higher priority unexpectedly requires an hour, it can easily be substituted for dusting without disrupting your entire schedule. The dust will wait for you!

When scheduling time slots, include the 30 minutes for needlepoint, yoga, exercise, whatever. And allot *only* 15 minutes for the tasks you have been avoiding. Reward yourself by taking five minutes or an hour or an afternoon to read a magazine, watch a "soap," or picnic with the children—whatever *you* want to do. You deserve a reward for having better organized your time.

5) *Try sleeping less.* I know, I know. You will say, "Do you mean five hours instead of six?" But if you have been managing to get enough sleep, rising half an hour before the children in the morning is half an hour of organization that can make your day.

6) *Take a nap.* O.K., so I just said try sleeping less. But many experienced mothers who rise at 7 a.m. find a nap refreshes their enthusiasm and their efficiency.

7) *Read child-care books like a magazine.* There are hundreds of books about children. You won't agree with them all, but they can offer good ideas. Use a

highlighter or keep your notebook handy as you skim them for information. Jot down ideas for easy reference when you need inspiration.

8) *Leave the house 10 minutes early.* Set your watch ahead if necessary, or write down appointment times earlier in your notebook. Being on time helps you control your life. A helpful hint: If you are going to a doctor or dentist who always keeps you waiting for hours, call ahead and ask if the doctor is on schedule or running late. Such a call will make sure you don't waste your time waiting for the professional whose services you have hired.

9) *Discover your best time of the day.* Time expert Lakein calls this our "prime time." Do your most important tasks then.

10) *Expect the unexpected.* Flexibility, thy name is mother. We may dream all night about what we would like to happen, but when the alarm clock rings, it's anybody's guess. That doesn't mean you are not in charge, however. It simply means accepting life's predictably unpredictable nature.

## De-Hasseling Housework

De-hasseling housework is a matter of determining which domestic tasks are drudgery and which are a source of personal satisfaction *for you.*

Again it is important to remember that we are speaking here of domestic skills, not mothering skills. So let's not confuse the ability to decorate a home, keep cupboards organized, or serve a luscious soufflé with our ability to create an emotionally supportive environment for our children.

Our child's fulfillment will neither be enhanced nor impaired because we cook like Julia Child or clean like a professional crew. Realize that you can be an excellent mother in spite of frozen TV dinners or dust bunnies under the bed.

Now that we have assured ourselves of that crucial difference, let's look at the options available to mothers when it comes to devoting time to household tasks.

Some of us like to cook—a lot! We consider it bliss to be surrounded by bubbling tomato sauce, crumb-crust pies and vegetables steamed to perfection. We would be horrified by the idea of serving frozen enchiladas, Doritos and Twinkies.

Some others get a warm glow when drawers are straightened, silver is polished, and every room has a place for everything and everything is in its place.

Fine—as long as we recognize that those priorities are a matter of choice, not dogma, and that we are free to devote our time to the things we enjoy most.

What happens to some of us, however, is that we decide we must do it *all* to perfection. We want to be a gourmet cook *and* keep our house looking like a page from *Better Homes and Gardens*. What we forget is that young children don't live on the pages of *Better Homes and Gardens* and Julia Child doesn't have a two-year-old hanging on her leg while she whips up a batch of Pasta Riviera. Mothers can be burdened with a large dose of guilt when they forget that perfection exists only in the mind of the perfectionist.

So let's admit that only God can achieve the impossible and look at our choices rationally: We have to admit that some domestic tasks we like, and some we do not.

### Exercise in Priority-Setting

Remember the old daisy routine, when we sat on a hillside, plucked the petals of a daisy and chanted, "He loves me, he loves me not"? We can treat our domestic options the same way. Homemakers are *not* predestined to carry out certain tasks for a certain number of hours every day.

Consider your role as a homemaker and the many tasks which can be a part of that role. Below, an assortment of household responsibilities forms the petals of a daisy. If you could pluck the petals one at a time— "I like it, I like it not"—which petals would you keep?

Add your own choices to the second daisy. Keep the jobs you like (add those we have forgotten) and take away the ones you don't like—creating your own unique way to blossom and grow.

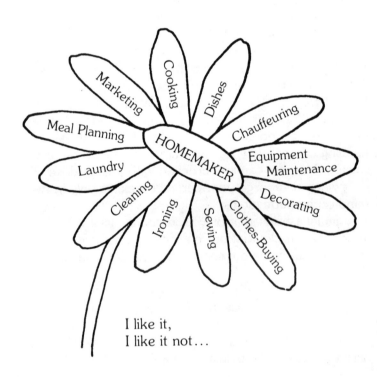

I like it,
I like it not...

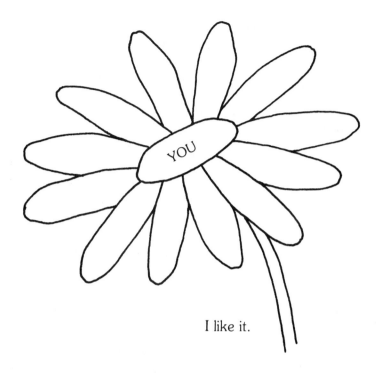

I like it.

After you've completed your own flower, you can concentrate on finding time for the tasks you enjoy. You can also sort the jobs you don't like into two categories: (1) tasks you don't like which must be done (cooking, cleaning, washing, etc.); (2) tasks you don't like which may not have to be done at all (ironing, sewing, chauffeuring, etc.).

Once you recognize the jobs you don't like which must be done, you have two more choices: Either find someone else to clean, wash and cook (a high school student in your neighborhood, someone you find from a newspaper ad, your own children or husband), or discover the fastest, easiest way for you to do those things yourself. Books and magazines are loaded with ideas, or you could ask other homemakers how they streamline such household activities.

It is also important to recognize the things you don't like to do which, with a little planning, may not have to be done at all. Buy wash-and-wear to avoid ironing; buy ready-to-wear and put the sewing machine away; organize a carpool or put the children on a bus and retire as chauffeur.

Once we become aware that there are choices to be made and options to consider in domestic tasks, no one should have to feel guilty because she doesn't do *everything* well.

## How to Fight Dirt(y)

No matter what our personal preferences in domestic tasks, we can all use a time-saving idea. Here are some suggestions other mothers say have worked for them:

1) *Schedule chores* according to daily, weekly, monthly or seasonal time slots. Know the enemy, and have a plan of attack.

2) *Divide and conquer.* Instead of tackling a whole closet, or washing all the windows, do one shelf a day or one window at a time.

3) *Have the longest phone cord in town.* Time experts say the telephone is one of our biggest time-wasters. But they only say that because their cords are too short! With a phone cord that reaches to the sink, other work areas and even other rooms, vital links with other adults can easily be maintained while you fold the laundry, clean the kitchen or straighten shelves—and never waste a minute.

4) *Put away knickknacks.* There will be less to dust, fewer things for the baby to break, and your house

will be in the height of style, since bare is currently beautiful in decorating.

5) *Do two things at one time.* Fold the laundry while you supervise your preschooler's coloring. Do the dishes while the toddler eats lunch. Take a nap while the baby naps.

6) *Keep a big wicker basket* in every room. It can hold toys so that, as you move from room to room during the day, the little ones can play with their things, not yours. Baskets can also hold magazines and other clutter when you want to clean up quickly.

7) *Limit the number of toys underfoot.* Store those which haven't been played with for a while. When you get them out again, they will seem like new.

8) *Don't make the beds.* Close the bedroom doors instead.

9) *Use shoe bags as organizers* for socks, underwear, small treasures. Install one on the inside door of your coat closet for mittens, hats and mufflers.

10) *Set aside one day a week to cook ahead* and freeze the results. It also helps to plan menus and shop for the whole week.

11) *Sit down while you prepare food* or iron— whenever possible—unless the toddler insists on sitting in your lap. (When *was* the last time you sat down?)

12) *Shop at odd times* like the dinner hour or early morning when lines are shorter.

13) *Trade money for time* (if possible and when necessary). Shop only in one store. You may not be able to get as many specials that way, but you save time. Arrange your list so you only have to go around the store once.

Convenience foods can be a real treat for the cook now and then. (Watch for preservatives. Frozen foods sometimes have fewer.) We all need a break, and the prepared foods you buy and fix at home are cheaper than a restaurant.

14) *Go to a restaurant* (when you can afford it). Nothing, but nothing, does a mother's heart more good than being served a meal with no responsibility for preparation and clean-up. And that freedom allows everyone to concentrate fully on the fun of being together.

15) *Whoever uses a plate should scrape it and put it in the dishwasher or sink.* Make this a rule as soon as the children are old enough. (Your husband is old enough.)

## Working Mothers

When it comes to a mother's time, one of the most controversial issues is where she should spend it.

Over half of married mothers with children now work outside their homes. As a 1980 issue of *Newsweek* reported, "The guilt, the goals, and the go-it-alone grind have become achingly familiar to millions of American women. They are trapped in the superwoman squeeze, the constant pressure to juggle home, family and job....For the first time in history, working wives outnumber housewives."

In that article Tina Oakland, director of the Women's Resource Center at the University of California says, "Now we get the jobs all right, *all* the jobs—at home, with the kids, and at work."

Besides having all the jobs, we get paid less than a man for doing them. Latest statistics show the average woman earns 59 percent of what a man earns, and only 17 percent of women belong to unions. Job status hasn't changed much either. Only six percent of women are in managerial/administrative positions.

One of the sad tensions of our age is that women

feel guilty if they take a job and guilty if they stay home. The truth is that either choice has advantages and drawbacks—both for mother and child. Additional income has to be weighed against expenses of transportation, clothing, lunches, taxes. A child whose mother is always there can find security in her presence or be smothered by it; a child whose mother works can be neglected or can reach responsible independence at an earlier age. The working mother will still bear the major responsibility for domestic chores, even though she assigns them to others; she will—sink or swim— learn to prioritize.

The way we choose to mother is a highly personal matter. In these days of double-digit inflation, full-time mothering is a luxury some of us cannot afford. As Betty Friedan once quipped during an interview, "If a mother is going to stay in the kitchen, who is going to pay for the bread?" But she added, "You cannot have it all (marriage, perfect family, perfect home, career)." She suggests less demanding housekeeping standards, pregnancy leave for working women, father and mother sharing both parenting and earning. Friedan says, "This sharing strengthens a family, has a humanizing force against all the dehumanizing factors in the world....But new families won't necessarily be the kind with the Good Housekeeping seal of approval."

Margaret Mead wrote, "Today the wife hopes— indeed expects— that her husband will be fully supportive of *her* choice of life-style, whether to stay at home with her children or, on the contrary, to combine marriage, motherhood and a full-time career."

One way to shared responsibility is through flex-time, an alternative schedule where workers tailor their own hours. Another consideration is the part-time job, or a full-time job shared with one or two other part-time employees. Some federal part-timers are now eligible to receive prorated benefits. Certain sectors of private industry have also initiated such programs.

In one midwestern city a public information specialist shares her full-time job with a teacher. She handles the daytime work while her daughter is in nursery school; the teacher handles assignments in the evenings and during the summer. "I wanted to continue my career, but I also wanted to raise my child myself," she said. "This has been a way to do both."

Perhaps the greatest concern of working mothers with young children is leaving those children. Often women feel that only they can give the special kind of care their children deserve. One mother commented, "Someone else will teach the eighth grade history. Nobody else will love my baby like I do."

The decision to take time out from a career to stay home and care for a child is not an easy one to make, according to pediatrician Sally Shaywitz. She says it is considered "unprofessional" in the working world to do so. She felt her colleagues accepted the premise that their own needs and those of their children must be subordinated to their work. There was admiring talk about how so-and-so worked up until two hours before delivery, and came back on the job six weeks later.

Her own experience showed that motherhood-by-telephone had its limitations. She found she could not schedule her child's critical moments between 5 and 9 p.m. "A child cannot program triumphs, injuries, worries to coincide with her mother's free time." To be there for those moments, however, a mother often sacrifices the status and rewards of a career—just as a mother who works must forego some of the rewards and joys of full-time mothering. Shaywitz makes the point that a mother's desire to raise her child herself should be taken out of the realm of "feminine whim" and recognized as a valid need.

Journalist Joyce Maynard speaks of being a professional writer as well as a mother: "It does seem to me that there's absolutely no way—no matter how many experts you consult—to predict how a child will change your life. There is only so much about skydiving you can learn on the ground. Past a point, confronting parenthood too, there is nothing for it but to jump. Once having jumped, though, no couple should think of going back, ever, to the way things used to be in their 'real life.' For myself, I never really pictured us as 'taking time out' to have Audrey. She is simply with us, and part of my advancement in my career as a person."

## Child Care

There is little definitive research on the effect day care has on children. Specialists say that good day care does not seem to have a negative effect, but beyond that each professional has his or her own advice. Child psychologist and researcher Burton White says that in the first year it is best if the mother works part-time and her hours overlap with naps as much as possible. Researcher-psychologist Jerome Kagan reversed his past opposition to day care after his recent study of a Harvard-operated center indicated such care does not harm the development of young children.

Of course there are child-care options besides day-care centers. There may be relatives who will watch your children. You can hire a professional baby-sitter who will come to your home. There are day-care homes where a mother watches several children at a time on a regular basis. Preschool programs can also offer mothers a block of time for outside career pursuits, or a mother might consider second- or third-shift work so that her husband can be with their children when she cannot.

Sometimes two mothers work part-time on different days of the week, trading child care on the days they are home. Other mothers find different solutions: Susan, the mother of a three- and four-year-old, shares the salary from her job as a key-punch operator with a neighbor, Karen, who watches Susan's children while she works. Karen needs the income but really enjoys being home with children, so this is a good solution for both of them.

There are also older people who would benefit from the company of children as well as from the extra income. One young mother who was returning to work posted a "baby-sitter wanted" ad at her local senior citizen center and talked to not one but five highly qualified persons.

It is important to investigate the people who are watching your children and for both you and your child to meet them personally before you hire them. Watch their interaction with your child and your child's reaction to them. Require at least three references and check those references thoroughly.

Psychologist Lee Salk cautions, "We don't mean to suggest that parents should never allow other people to look after their children. What we *are* suggesting is that parents choose these people carefully. Many people...will hire any able-bodied person to be with their children, for hours at a time, day after day, as though it made no difference to the development of the child's capacities. But it does."

There are many books and much informaiton available to help select excellent day care. If you are looking for that alternative it will be helpful to read as much as possible. Quality day care means care-givers who are patient, flexible, firm yet kind, who enjoy being with children and have values similar to your own. The home or center where the child stays should offer ample opportunity for the physical and mental, social and emotional development of children.

A day-care center should have a good adult-to-child ratio, meet the requirements of the Board of Health and be licensed where required. Above all, parents should be encouraged to observe the day-care center any time. Go often and unannounced. Look carefully at the children, the employees, the program—and be objective about the care they offer.

It also seems important to stick with a good selection of child care once you have made it. Young children are forming important attachments in the early years and it is better for them not to be moved many times from place to place.

Despite other differences, researchers do agree on two points about mothers and their children: (1) It is not so much whether a mother works, but rather what kind of alternative care is provided that is important to the well-being of the child. (2) A mother and her children both seem happiest and mentally healthiest when the mother is doing what she wants to do, whether working or remaining at home.

**Time and Time Again**

Young children are very much influenced by their parents, and we want to influence them. Our children are our gift to humanity. We want to give them the part of ourselves that will help them be most uniquely themselves. That part of us will be their heritage; it's something only a family can give, regardless of who works when or where, inside or outside the home.

Time is not only the name of this chapter, it is the name of life. Managing our time and our lives is one of the greatest challenges we will ever face. Time-management techniques can seem complicated. But managing our time is as simple as understanding what is important to us, and using our time to make it happen. It can mean taking the time to listen to our child's latest adventure, taking the time to read that novel we have been promising ourselves, or simply taking the time to say, "I love you." No matter what our schedule, we can make every single moment count.

## For Discussion and Awareness

1) How well do you manage your time? What aspect of dealing with your time is the biggest problem for you?

2) What are your "A" priorities at this time in your life? What will you do *today* to achieve those priorities?

3) When you were a child and people asked what you wanted to be when you grew up, what was your answer? Have you fulfilled that or any dream in your life?

4) Do you schedule time for the hobbies, interests and activities that you personally enjoy?

5) Which domestic tasks are a source of pride and satisfaction for you? Name one household task that you could do less often.

6) Do you work in a profession besides motherhood? Full- or part-time? Are you comfortable with that life-style? What are its advantages? Drawbacks?

7) Is quality day care available in your area? What day-care alternatives have worked well for you or people you know?

## Idea for Action

Talk to all the members of your family and decide on a
leisure-time activity you can all enjoy together. Then set
aside the time to enjoy it!

## Bibliography

Bee, Helen. *The Developing Child.* New York: Harper and
    Row, 1978.
Bombeck, Erma. *At Wit's End.* New York: Doubleday, 1967.
Drucker, Peter. *The Effective Executive.* New York:
    Harper and Row, 1966.
Lakein, Alan. *How to Get Control of Your Time and Your
    Life.* New York: Signet, 1974.
Langway, Lynn, *et al.* "The Superwoman Squeeze."
    *Newsweek* (May 19, 1980), pp. 72-79.
Maynard, Joyce. "My Career as a Mother." *Newsweek*
    (July 17, 1978), p. 18.
Mead, Margaret, and Rhoda Metraux. "A Better Mother,
    a Better Wife, a Better Person." *Redbook* (February,
    1979), p. 46.
*Quality Day Care (What to Look For; How to Get
    It!),* Family Development and Management Series.
    Frankfort, Kentucky: Kentucky State University,
    October, 1976.
Salk, Lee, Ph.D., and Rita Kramer. *How to Raise a Human
    Being.* New York: Warner Books, 1969.
Shaywitz, Sally E., M.D. "Baby Doctor Challenges the Part-
    Time Mother." *The Cincinnati Enquirer* (May 7, 1973),
    p. 22.
White, Burton, Ph.D. *The First Three Years of Life.*
    New Jersey: Prentice-Hall, 1975.
Whitebread, Jane. "Who's Taking Care of the Children?"
    *Family Circle* (February 20, 1979), p. 88.

To love someone is to give that person
credit for having more than we have
found in him.... To love someone is to
have unending hope in him.

—Louis Evely
*Lovers in Marriage*

# Chapter 6
# Marriage: Survival Tactics

Being wildly, wonderfully, totally and forever in love
is no problem—on your honeymoon. After that it gets
more complicated. When you have children, things
become even more complex.

Mothers and fathers are full-time lovers. Without
love babies die, children wither, marriages crumble.
Sometimes we parents become so preoccupied with the
proper methods of raising children that we forget how

many parental imperfections one hug can wipe away. Physician Michael Miller reminds us, "Love has brought more children to happy adulthood than technique."

Psychiatrist Aaron Stern agrees. He claims that a child-centered home is destructive to the child. Rather, he says, it is the love between parents which should be the center of the home. The parental love children witness then becomes something they can aspire to— something they later leave the home to achieve themselves.

**Models for Marriage**

There are currently many formats which promise to keep love alive. One approach is the kind of supportive relationship where both partners try to give more than 50 percent. Each person in such a relationship is dedicated to helping the other reach fulfillment.

Another model is Marabel Morgan's *Total Woman*. She says, "A great marriage is not so much finding the right person, as *being* the right person." With this technique a wife offers no criticism or disagreement, only admiration and support.

Then there is "open marriage." No, open marriage does not mean an open-door policy on sexual relationships as the popular misconception would imply.

Open marriage encourages separate experiences and choices, an end to the "togetherness" myth which claims a couple is not only "two in one flesh" but two in one's set of friends, hobbies and habits as well. Open marriage includes equality, trust and flexibility of roles.

Jerome Folkman, a rabbi, marriage counselor and professor of sociology at Ohio State University, proposes another formula for success. He tells couples to have the wedding—then forget it. His suggestion:

"Just act like you're not married at all. Keep right on being lovers."

It is interesting that we are considered "lovers" before marriage, "husband and wife" after. Perhaps that odd turn of events accounts for the current spiraling divorce rate.

Each of these models works for someone. What is important is that we be personally creative about what works for the people in *our* marriage.

Marriage is a unique act of love because it happens between two unique people. Each marriage is a union unlike any other that has ever happened before, unlike any that will ever happen again.

In *Lovers in Marriage*, Louis Evely says the first obligation of a married couple is "to be alive." He says few of us consider this obligation. In Evely's words, "A home is not destroyed by quarrels, by unforeseen difficulties, by money crises, or even by infidelity. What destroys a home is the rut of routine. When, without realizing it, you stop looking at each other, or talking to each other, or quarreling with each other, then the household is in danger."

Does the routine part of our marriage outweigh the thrill of surprise and discovery? That is the critical question! Sometimes we feel we know everything there is to know about our partner. By making that judgment we end all surprises and lose hope.

Marriage without hope is only cohabitation, just as surely as sex without love is lust. A living marriage increases the confidence and respect of both husband and wife. They are good for each other. They are good for themselves. They are best friends.

**Being Best Friends**
True friends are easy to recognize—they reinforce

us. They don't tell us what they think we want to hear; they tell us what they think we should hear. They comfort us when we fail. They congratulate us when we win. Friends defend us in our absence as well as our presence. They offer affection, compassion and wisdom.

Best friends are a loyal, loving connection with life. Marriage demands such connections, and the real survivors are those who not only accept that challenge, but thrive on it.

How can you and your husband be best friends? Here are a few ideas about friendship between lovers.

1) *Accept limitations.* Limitations are a part of the human condition. If your husband's goal is executive success, his business may mean lonely nights for you and the children. Or he may be a great family man who seems to have little career ambition. We often forget that what attracted us to him in the first place is probably that very drive or casualness. Help him understand your feelings, and be aware of his possibilities. But don't get so caught up in what could be that you waste the beauty of what is.

2) *Help each other grow.* It's called staying alive. Know your expectations. Know his expectations. And know you can change—*yourselves.* Your husband *can* stop smoking. You *can* learn to relax. But only if you each want to.

How you go about helping each other change is what is important. No one likes orders, ultimatums or sermons. Everyone likes being heard, understood and nourished with support.

3) *Come to grips with reality.* Realize that marriage carries with it as much false advertising as motherhood. Learn to separate fact from fiction. Marriage will not cure loneliness (there are times when you will be apart). Marriage will not fulfill all your needs (name anything

that will). There are no happily-ever-afters. Marriage is not the end of a story; it is the beginning.

4) *Kick the role habit.* Friends don't force each other into molds. Forget the stereotypes—the way your parents did it, what the neighbors will think. Who does the dishes, who cuts the grass, who cares for the children and who washes the dog are not a matter of divine revelation. Who *wants* to is what is important.

5) *Share pain, share happiness.* In the first case we diminish the hurt; in the second we intensify the joy. Enhance each other's lives with your own experiences. Everybody wants to be a part of someone who is turned on to life.

6) *Retire from the "Pepsi Generation."* Nobody stays young forever, so why pretend we will? Give each other permission to age well. Forget the Peter Pan propaganda and enjoy the warmth, wisdom, and experience which being over 30 brings.

7) *Don't overestimate sex.* Sure sex is great, but it is one part of marriage, not the alpha and the omega. There will be times when sex is a disappointment—it's too early, it's too late, the baby's crying. There can be role conflicts (parent vs. person), times of abstinence, times of sickness, times of "I just don't feel like it" for both of you.

And why should that surprise us? That is how it is with everything else in life—our job, our family, our state of mind.

Yet when sex is less than perfect, we panic. We fear the romance is gone forever. Still, every writer on the subject from Carl Rogers to Masters and Johnson says that sex in a healthy marriage improves with time. So be gentle with yourselves. If there is a special problem, talk to a professional. Meanwhile, keep on loving each other patiently, carefully—and whenever possible.

8) *Respect each other.* Being best friends is basically a matter of common sense and kindness. It involves things like showing gratitude, respecting privacy, developing a sense of humor. It also involves taking care of ourselves so that others don't have to devote their lives to taking care of us.

Writer Shirley Streshinsky sums it up like this:

> The good marriage is somewhat like a trapeze act. To begin with, it requires a certain aptitude, a basic wish to work with one other person in some death-defying venture. Then it takes a lot of good practice before the real soaring begins. Success requires each partner to be independent, to be strong in a critical way, to be responsible for the unit. Through trust and timing and a certain tension, each can help the other reach new heights. Or just enjoy the flying.

## Learning to Communicate

Basic to friendship is keeping in touch, and that involves communicating. But communication is more than the words we say: "You won't be home for dinner tonight?"

Communication is also the frown on our face, the irritation in our voice, and the fact that we tense up while saying it—all of which speak as loudly as our words.

Each of us communicates in a unique language which is made up of past experiences, biases and emotions. To communicate fully we must listen to what a person *isn't* saying just as surely as we listen to what he is saying.

*The words of the message are:* "The boss asked me to stay late and work on my presentation for tomorrow."

*But the speaker really means:* "I'm so tired, I don't know how I'm going to do this. But if that meeting fails, I fail. And then where will we get money to put food on the table?"

*While the listener hears:* "He's not coming home again. I don't know why I even bother to fix a decent dinner. He doesn't appreciate it. Why should he when he has the pick of any restaurant in town? Besides it's certainly more peaceful eating without the kids. I wish I could work late—anywhere but here!"

In his book *Why Am I Afraid to Tell You Who I Am?*, John Powell says there are five levels of communication which can tell us how willing we are to reveal ourselves to others. Strangers can only converse on level five; lovers/friends reach level one.

Level five is *cliche conversation*. It's the cocktail party chit-chat we know so well: "How are you?" "How are the children?" "Have a good day." It's the kind of statement many people make, but few really think about. In a marriage, this kind of communication builds more walls than bridges.

Level four is *reporting the facts about others*. Again, we offer nothing of ourselves, only the latest news, neighborhood gossip, a story we have heard. Not much give, not much take.

Level three is *our ideas and judgments*. Here we begin to expose our real selves, but very cautiously. We may start to explain our judgment about working mothers, but if our husband gives even the slightest indication of displeasure, disagreement or boredom, we quickly change the subject. On this level we are interested in pleasing others.

On level two, we begin to speak *our feelings*. It is gut-level revelation, sharing the emotions which are individually our own. It means explaining the *feelings*

107

behind your wish to go back to work—and even more than that, your frustration, anxiety and sadness at the thought of not being home full-time.

Most of us fear others will not accept such emotional candor and so we avoid it, settling for the kind of superficiality which results in few disagreements, but little authentic communication. Real friends have no such fears.

Level one is *peak communication.* This kind of communication involves intellectual and emotional communion. We reach out so that our feelings are *experienced* by the other person.

Peak communication under the best circumstances is an art. Such sharing in the midst of calming a colicky baby and the cross-examination of a three-year-old is a miracle.

And yet peak communication is a given in a living marriage. It grows out of those nights before we were married when we talked until dawn. It can be achieved again. Here are a few ground rules to set the scene for such intimacy:

1) *Stop what you're doing.* If either of you has a concern that needs talking about *now,* leave the dishes in the sink, give the baby a bottle, look your husband in the eye and say, "Let's talk for awhile."

2) *Don't crowd each other.* Sometimes silence is the kindest form of communication. If possible, allow both of you the needed space to unwind from the pressure of the day before your conversation becomes just another demand. Timing is crucial in productive communication.

3) *Be nice for at least four minutes.* Leonard Zunin, M.D., says that one of the most critical times for a married couple is the first four minutes when they are reunited at the end of a working day. This reunion,

Zunin says, will often set the mood of the entire evening not only for husband and wife but for the rest of the family as well.

Picture your own home at that time. What is the atmosphere? Do you smile? Do your eyes meet? Is your hair combed? Less than half the messages sent out at this time are spoken; the rest are given through body language.

4) *Listen for feelings.* Norma Randolph Anderson in her "Self-Enhancing Education" workshops calls this "reflective listening." When the person you love is telling you how he feels, encourage him to continue. Do not advise or judge, criticize or blame. In Anderson's words, "Let him take you where it hurts."

To complete the exchange, be responsible for communicating your own feelings. Send "I" messages: "I feel hurt" instead of "You hurt me." "I'm really angry!" instead of "You make me so mad!" Haim Ginott explains that the cardinal principle in communication is, "Talk to the situation, not to the personality and character."

Two people are most likely to reach an impasse when both are hurting so much that neither one is able to hear what the other must say.

5) *Put aside time for being together.* Schedule couple-time for just the two of you on a regular basis. Make a kind of night out at home. Put routine activity aside: Nobody works on a report, nobody does mending, nobody changes the oil. One young couple sets aside every Thursday evening as their own. They put the children to bed early, have a candlelight dinner and savor the evening and each other.

6) *Think about what you want to say.* Instead of simply dumping the last month's accumulation of worries and frustrations on the other person, do some preliminary thinking. Try to write down facts, concerns

and goals. When you come together to talk you can use your creative energy to answer the question you have identified instead of spending hours trying to define it.

7) *Love each other.* One husband told his wife during an argument, "How can we talk to each other like this? How can one problem make us forget all the great things that have happened for the last nine years?"

Sometimes the passion of the moment makes us forget all the passion that brought us to this moment in the first place. Love includes understanding that we are the most significant person in our husband's life, just as he is in ours. Love also includes communicating that fact often, and with feeling.

8) *Pray together.* Lovers need each other and they need God. We all ask ourselves who we are, where we are going, what we are doing here and what difference does it make anyway? Sometimes we do not need to talk but to listen—to the Lord.

Marriage is full of celebration—our joy in each other, the birth of a child, a promotion, buying our own home. Marriage also knows sadness—sickness, loss, financial trouble, the tedium of life itself.

It is that celebration and suffering which we can bring to God—and leave in his hands.

## Fathering

Fathering is easy to define. It is the same as mothering, except for the sex of the participant. This book is about mothering—parenting from a woman's perspective—because, currently, most full-time parents are women. Today it is mostly women who deal with the confused identity, isolation and loss of status which comes with full-time responsibility for a child. Men faced with that same responsibility would—and do—respond similarly.

What is a father? Technically, he is a male parent. But society defines him much like television interviewer Phil Donahue defined himself in his autobiography: "Fatherhood, I thought, was a natural responsibility that required no training and could be discharged in the evenings."

What is a mother? Technically, she is a female parent. But society defines her as the person chiefly responsible for the care and training of children. Society says that what comes naturally to the woman is not necessary in the man. Society lies.

We all know fathers who not only have had one heck of a good time making the baby, but who have one heck of a good time caring for her as well. We also know divorced, separated or widowed fathers who are primarily responsible for loving and encouraging their young children. Obviously fathers can be "mothers," too.

The key to success for any person who is in the business of loving and living with young children is nurturance. "Nurturance, the ability to protect and comfort a child, has been an undervalued facet of masculinity in our society," say Henry Biller and Dennis Meredith in their book *Father Power.*

According to Margaret Mead, no anthropological evidence gives women an edge in nurturing. In fact, her studies of other cultures suggest that the child adjusts most easily when "...cared for by many warm, friendly people."

Multiple mothering was studied in an Israeli kibbutz and later at Harvard by psychologist Milton Kotelchuck. He observed that fathers are an important part of a child's nurturance. "They're always there, they help out in time of need, they share educative tasks." His research showed infants respond similarly to fathers and

111

mothers. Babies will protest the departure of either parent, but not the departure of a stranger. The child could be equally comforted by either parent.

Such mutual concern, however, is not automatic. Both parents must want to make it happen. And in the early years, both will have to strive to be less work-centered. In *Life Without Fathering* Maureen Green says, "Everyone can benefit from the reinvention of family roles. Mother is being recognized as a person, and as a person who can think. Father must be recognized as a person, and as a person who can feel."

## More Myths

Men are currently subjected to as much indoctrination about fatherhood and masculinity as women are about motherhood and femininity. The myths include:

1) *Real men never show emotion or affection, especially with their sons.* The imagined risk is that such behavior will make the child weak and effeminate (forgivable, even desirable traits in girls). Research shows a different effect: The most secure children are those whose fathers express affection freely and model emotion for both sons and daughters.

2) *A father is a figurehead; mothers mold the children.* Again, we are accepting stereotypes about pink for girls and blue for boys, confusing mothering with parenting. Children will learn. The parent who makes the difference is the parent who wants to.

3) *Fathers aren't cut out for parenthood; they don't have a mother's instinct.* Sorry to break it to you, Dad, but Mom doesn't have a "mother's instinct" either. Parenthood—motherhood and fatherhood—is a learning process. Like any skill, it requires information and experience. As psychologist Fitzhugh Dodson says: "My

clinical impression is that both mothers and fathers start out equally ignorant about babies and small children. Mothers eventually learn something about them by sheer trial and error. Fathers are not even that fortunate. And that's where the tragedy lies."

## Token Dad-ism

The popular trend is for fathers to be involved with their children superficially, to give an outward appearance of nurturance. The father will help his wife by giving an occasional bottle, changing an occasional diaper, caring for the children on an occasional evening.

Several factors make it difficult for some mothers to encourage such on-again, off-again involvement:

1) *She may feel guilty.* ("He works all day at the office.")

2) *He may make her feel guilty.* ("Had a helluva day.")

3) *He may make her mad.* (Father comes in, kisses baby dutifully, then has a beer and falls asleep on the couch.)

4) *She may be reluctant to share the power of the home.* ("This is one place where *I'm* in charge.")

It's not that women can't use or don't want the help. It's more that they can't depend on it. Sociologist Jessie Bernard says, "Just helping, which does not relieve the mother of any of her responsibilities, is therefore not enough. A helper can relieve the mother but can also renege or cop out. Making sure the service is performed can be as wearing as performing it oneself. And being held responsible for its actual performance is the hardest part of all."

True fatherhood requires commitment, not image. It is a full-time sharing, whenever and however possible— for the duration. It is the kind of support which means

113

sustaining a mother intellectually and emotionally as well as physically. It frees a mother because she is sure that she shares, not just bears, responsibility for the children.

How each couple goes about this sharing (written lists, verbal agreements, day-by-day decisions) is, like parenthood itself, a matter of what works. How it happens is not nearly so important as *that* it happens.

A father's ability to help his wife can be limited by economics, time and preference. But his ability to support her in the sense of accepting real responsibility for his child's continuous development is only as limited as the father himself.

A father can take his son fishing one weekend a year, or he can talk to that child and become involved with him every single day of his life. A father can change the baby when the mother is at the end of her rope, or he can interact intimately with his child from the moment of birth and every available moment thereafter. That's support. That's shared responsibility. And that's what makes a parent of either sex effective.

Shared parenthood is easiest when the father learns about nurturing from pregnancy on. Childbirth classes with involvement for both parents help. Dad in the delivery room is an experience most men report really makes this "our" baby. So does lots of freedom for the new father to care for the child in the hospital and at home.

It is vital that both parents share their child's life. It is vital to the growth of the child; it is vital to the growth of the parent. If we don't allow, encourage, insist on our husband's support, he may simply go back to his old ways out of habit—and miss fatherhood altogether. And who has the right to let that happen to a very best friend?

Lovers who are also parents share themselves and

their children in a marriage. Such a commitment is courageous. It involves complications, crises, failures and feelings. As husband and wife, we need trust and honesty; we need self-confidence and realistic objectives; we need communication and forgiveness. But the real magic in a marriage is the two of us. Because, more than anything, we need each other.

## For Discussion and Awareness

1) Do you think it's more difficult to be married and stay married in society today than it was 50 years ago? Why?

2) How is being married different than you thought it would be before you were married? Were there any disappointments? Any pleasant surprises?

3) Think of a time in your marriage that you consider one of the very best. What made it that way?

4) Do you and your husband talk often and on a regular basis? What could you do to improve communication in your marriage?

5) Is your husband an involved father? What can you do to encourage your husband's involvement with the children?

6) At what times do you best communicate with your husband?

## Idea for Action

Make plans to attend a Marriage Encounter Weekend with your husband.

# Bibliography

Bernard, Jessie. *The Future of Motherhood.* New York: Dial, 1974.

Billner, Henry, Ph.D., and Dennis Meredith. *Father Power.* New York: Doubleday, 1975.

Dodson, Fitzhugh, Ph.D. *How to Father.* New York: Signet Books, 1974.

Donahue, Phil, and Company. *Donahue, My Own Story.* New York: Simon and Schuster, 1979.

Evely, Louis. *Lovers in Marriage.* New York: Herder and Herder, 1968.

Ginott, Haim. *Teacher and Child.* New York: The Macmillan Company, 1972.

Gornick, Vivian. "How Important Is a Father to His Child?" *Family Circle* (April, 1974), p. 52.

Green, Maureen. *Life Without Fathering.* New York: McGraw-Hill, 1976.

Lamb, Michael. "Fathers: Forgotton Contributors to Child Development." *Human Development* (Volume 18, 1975), pp. 245-266.

Miller, Michael. *Sunday's Child.* New York: Holt, Rinehart, and Winston, 1968.

Morgan, Marabel. *The Total Woman.* New Jersey: Revell, 1973.

Masters, William H., and Virginia E. Johnson. *The Pleasure Bond.* Boston: Little, Brown and Company, 1974.

O'Neill, Nena and George. *Open Marriage.* New York: Avon Books, 1972.

Powell, John. *Why Am I Afraid to Tell You Who I Am?* Niles, Illinois: Argus Communications, 1969.

Rogers, Carl R., Ph.D. *Becoming Partners.* New York: Delacorte Press, 1972.

Streshinsky, Shirley. "Beyond Love: The Special Rewards of Marriage." *Redbook* (May, 1974), p. 95.

Zunin, Leonard, M.D., with Natalie Zunin. *Contact: The First Four Minutes*. New York: Ballantine Books, 1975.